CW01311037

SARAH BULLEN

LOVE AND ABOVE

A JOURNEY INTO SHAMANISM, COMA AND MAGIC

Published by
Tafelberg, an imprint of NB Publishers,
a division of Media24 Books Pty (Ltd),
40 Heerengracht, Cape Town, South Africa
www.tafelberg.com

Copyright © Sarah Bullen

All rights reserved. No part of this publication may be reproduced or transmitted, in any form or by any means, without prior permission from the publisher or copyright holder.

Set in 11,5 on 16,5 Garamond
Cover design by Melanie Kriel
Typesetting by Clare-Rose Julius
Edited by Angela Voges
Proof read by Lathleen Sutton and Eugenie du Preez
Author photograph on back cover by Alix Rose
www.thewritingroom.co.za

ISBN: 979-8-82455-359-8

Here is the world.
Beautiful and terrible things will happen.
Don't be afraid.
— Frederick Buechner

To Llewelyn, and those both seen and unseen that guide us on our journey to love.

CONTENTS

Author's note 9

The madness begins 13

PART 1: Tumour, shamanism and wildness
    It started with sex 23
    The film director 34
    The sangoma journey 45
    Prepare for brain removal 50
    Phakalane Centre for Ritual 56
    Fear: I know you well, old friend 62
    A missing piece of brain 64
    My magazine goes bust 66
    Navigating conspiracy and cancer 68
    Greeting the ancestors 70
    The bika ceremony 74
    Gathering the drums and throwing the bones 78
    The sangoma's dance 82
    The Naked Man medicine 89
    Wild rapture 93
    King of the Congo again 100
    Air initiation ceremony 103
    Holy smoke and spirits 110
    The big news dinner 117

PART 2: The coma
    The endgame 125
    The magazine boss 128
    An epic freefall 133
    Coma stage 1: The world of nightmares 135
    Stage 2: Out of the body 138
    Stage 3: Limbo 141
    Stage 4: The ceremony to say goodbye 143
    Stage 5: Floating away 148

Stage 6: The house at the end of the world 151
Stage 7: The spirit guide comes 154
Stage 8: Waking up 158

PART 3: Carve the doors with bones and flesh

Dream fever 165
The ICU torture chamber 173
The countdown begins 175
I learn to walk 182
One last goodbye 186
Overcoat 191
Survival mode 193
Post-traumatic bliss 196
Love and above 203
The vow 207

PART 4: Greek island life

Lesbians, sex and sannyasins 211
Wild, wild country 218
Seduced into the love of life 226
Pulling the kids out of school 233
Open the seven gates 236
Village of mystics and magic 242
Cold winter for Shirley Valentine 247
It's hard to be a hippy with kids 250
Summer life's a beach 254
The lesbian festival organiser 256
The Greek musician 259
The path of love 265
The Resurrection Plant 267

Afterword – a new cancer journey 269

Acknowledgements 274

About the author 277

AUTHOR'S NOTE

This was such a tightly focused story that so much had to be left behind. But I was lucky to be able to allow Llewelyn to speak from the grave, in his own voice. His diary entries are clearly marked in the text, and come directly from his blog 'Travels in hyperreality'. They still exist, floating out there on the internet, a record of a life lived.

I have changed very few names in the telling of the tale, and left them out entirely if anything could offend. Nothing in this book is intended to hurt anyone – either by its omission or by its inclusion. I apologise in advance if it does.

People say that what we're all seeking is a meaning for life. I don't think that's what we're really seeking. I think that what we're seeking is an experience of being alive, so that our life experiences on the purely physical plane will have resonances with our own innermost being and reality, so that we actually feel the rapture of being alive.

– Joseph Campbell

The madness begins

What am I doing here? It's an easy Sunday morning and I am sitting on a cold concrete floor with my legs stretched out in front of me and a six-kilogram black cock on the top my head.

I really *should not* be here.

I am a frazzled, but reasonably mature, hip and working mother of two small kids at age 34. And Sundays are rest and wine days.

I should be at my parents' house by the beach in Simonstown looking out over the yachts sailing. Soon I should be sitting down for a Sunday roast with a chilled glass of white wine. Or shouting as I chase my kids across the beach.

This cold hard floor is not the right place for me.

And yet here I am. Sitting quiet and meek with my head bowed and a cloth over my shoulders. I want to shift and move, but I don't dare.

Behind me a chant rises and the air begins to swirl. The weight of the cock is immense. It's resting on my head and getting heavier with every breath.

No! It's not that kind of cock.

Not the fun kind.

This is type with feathers and claws. And those claws are gripping my skull like a fork. I feel as if I cannot bear it one more second.

Not just the chicken and its groping feet, but this entire 'ceremony'.

Then chicken is lifted off and I could almost float with lightness and relief. I can't see what is happening behind me but I can hear the frenzied clucking and feel the sweep of the feathers against my back.

LOVE AND ABOVE

The wings drum against my head as it struggles to right itself.

I move to stand up.

'Right, I think I am done,' I gasp.

'Don't move.'

I feel that chicken being swung around and around my head in circles as the sangoma (shaman) standing behind me starts to chant and call.

He is calling to the ancestors, talking to them in a tongue I both know and don't know.

The fresh croissant I scoffed from the buzzing bakery down the road an hour earlier is threatening to come back up and out.

Around and around me the chicken goes.

I am feeling dizzy now, and disorientated.

Now two cocks are circling me. Oh hell, he has one in each hand – held by their feet – and they are being swung around and around my head in faster and faster circles. Their flapping, frantic wings are scraping my face, tiny pieces of down and dust are coating the air. I do not move.

I try not to breathe.

I think I am allergic to feathers. Certainly dust, as a sneeze looms.

I sit frozen, not daring to sneeze, alone in the centre of this wild display.

But I am not alone. Next to me sits my husband, his legs outstretched. It's my Llewelyn. Father of our two small children. The man I met at a party with the blondest of hair and the loudest of laughs. The crazy filmmaker who was the sexiest man in any room.

My heart beat faster the moment he walked up to me that very first night we met, almost a decade before, with a cocky smile and a cowboy hat. I am still not sure if it's ever beaten the same since.

It sure is beating fast now as we sit together on the cold floor with those massive birds swinging around our heads.

We are side by side, but worlds apart.

The madness begins

He is in rapture. I am terrified.

I don't dare look at him. I can only see him in my peripheral vision, but I don't need to see him to know what he is thinking. I don't want to look at him.

I know things about him just through tiny movements I can pick up. I know that his legs are shaking. Not because he is scared but because they have been stretched out straight for so long. He battles to sit for long. His muscles and joints have been weakened by three years of chemotherapy, so this position is a huge physical effort for him.

I know that he is focused and clear. He would never ask for it to end, or to take a break from the endless sitting.

This is a ritual and we must obey.

I know that he wants this ceremony; it is a ritual wash to bring us closer as a couple.

His eyes are closed and his lips move in the chant.

I make sure to keep mine open. Defiant and angry.

I know if I close them my already-thin grip on reality may be lost. I tried that earlier during a chant, I closed my eyes because it just felt right.

And then I wasn't sure of anything.

Not of who I was. Or where I was sitting. I felt suspended in air – a soul without ground to call home. And then it was so very hard to get them back open and find my way back into that room on that Sunday morning. I wasn't going to do it again.

'I think I want to go home.'

That is the only sentence in my mind right now. It stretches out before me like a neon sign over an exit in a dark, seedy street.

'I want to go home.'

I whisper it now.

Anything to escape the intensity of the moment.

Anything to escape the intensity of my life right now.

Anything to make sure the tumour in my husband's head does

not grow back. Again.

Anything that can make sense of the raw ache of grief I have pushed far away just so life can go on.

Anything to break out of this numbness of distance.

Anything to make sure he lives. Or that he dies and finally ends this long, strangling, crushing hold before it takes me down too.

Anything it takes.

'I want to go home.'

I speak louder now, but the noises surround me, and my voice is lost in the singing and chanting and those claws and wings.

The chickens are swirling faster now, creating a vacuum that sucks out the air in the room around me. I am locked in the sheer physicality of the experience. My sides are being battered by the huge wings as they swing around and around me. My already crazy curly blonde hair has escaped its tie and is standing up with what must look like static electricity.

We are here to do a ritual and a ceremony to thank our ancestors ahead of his next brain scan. Although the scans have happened with solid and unavoidable regularity, this next scan is something special.

After three years clear, an MRI has showed a rapid regrowth of his brain tumour.

So here we both sit.

I know what is going to come next – both chickens will be ritually killed out in the backyard. I will have to bathe in the blood later. I was told this ahead of time.

I grew up on a smallholding with many animals so killing chickens is that is not a big deal for me. Bathing in the blood, however, feels a step further.

I know that this ritual will end soon. We are in the final stages of a series of medicine baths and washes that we have been doing since early in the morning.

This last one is to call in beauty and joy.

The madness begins

This is nothing new to me. My husband has been studying with a sangoma for three years now and ritual and ceremony are very much part of our lives. He is studying to be a koma doctor – a doctor of rituals.

As much a part as the days spent in oncology wards and the interminable wait for the MRI results.

But this particular ritual is an unexpected crossroads for me.

I want out. Out of this room, out of this life.

I know all the people in this room. All four of us. I know them all intimately.

My husband I have known for nine years, two children and three years of brain cancer. His sangoma baba (father) is a trusted teacher and a friend. The other sangoma assisting in this ritual is a woman, healer and ritual specialist.

As the air moves faster and the chants get louder, the absurd thought crosses my mind that I am going to just get up and run. Not right now, that would be too obvious. But as soon as I get a gap and everybody is otherwise occupied, I am going to grab my clothes and bag and slip out the front door, walk to the main road just below the house, get into a taxi and drive away. From everything.

I will need to grab my clothes as I am currently naked and covered only with a hiya – a type of cotton sarong used for ritual. It is about to get covered with chicken blood.

But there is no running.

Not from this room.

Not from my marriage.

Not from the brain tumour that is back.

Nor from the costs that are piling up.

Not from my two children who need me.

Not from the death that is coming.

Running is for pussies who can't take the heat and I am not a pussy. So, I will stand in the fire with him.

LOVE AND ABOVE

I also know I am not going to run because the metal gate at the front door is double-locked. I checked it earlier when I tried to slip out. I can't get out. I am literally locked in.

Part 1

Tumour, shamanism and wildness

It started with sex

It was Saturday night three years earlier. We were on an Easter holiday, the kids were away and we were going to get it ON! We had a big mortgage, two cars we were paying off and two small toddlers, and basically hadn't had sex for months.

Pretty much because I hated him. That's normal in any marriage, right?

Family holidays with toddlers really are the pits, so we hit on the bright idea of combining an Easter holiday at the coast with a lovers' dirty weekend. We would drive halfway across the country, closer to the grandparents, and then send the kids off with them for two days. Perfect solution.

His parents lived two hours away, and they arrived and spent a night with us. The next day they packed up and drove home, the kids in the back.

Freedom. We were going to be naughty for three delicious days. We would sleep late, drink tequila (me, not him) and fuck like we were 28 again – before we had kids.

Except we weren't really rocking the dirty weekend part. Our marriage was rocky, and we were in the middle of a perpetual squabble that had lasted three years. The fight was about many things: not enough money, the stress of small children and another, more complex, one. I wanted a third child, and he did not.

He'd said 'hell no' three years ago when I had first raised it. And he'd kept saying no every time I'd asked. But things had come to a head that January. We had taken a relaxing holiday – a week sharing a small canoe and shooting rapids on the Orange River. The adventure holiday was spent in a continual state of war.

'You are not pulling hard enough,' he would grunt, sweat beading off his back. 'Erm, yes, correct. I am taking a small break. Having a sip of water. Is that a problem?'

'Swap places so I can watch your strokes,' he demanded.

'You are surely joking?'

'No. It's clear you have no rhythm; I am going to sit at the back and tap the beat on your back with my foot . . . see if you can stick to it.'

'How about I take this oar, snap a sharp edge and stick it through your leg?'

'Okay guys,' the river guide laughed nervously. 'Let's try and work as a team. Divorces have happened on this river.'

That night the bickering came to a head.

'Yes or no?' I asked.

'Yes or no what?'

'Another baby, of course,' I said. 'I need a final answer. Can we have another baby?' Men can be so thick.

'Nooo!' he roared. 'N. O.'

He then lifted an impressively sized boulder, tossed it and went into a series of striking blows on a nearby tree. I feigned disinterest.

Tall, blonde and well-built, he was powerful and impressive. His hair was cut short and edgy, which reflected his attitude. At 36 he was a top commercials and music video director, celebrated for his filmmaking and his style. Quirky, Afrikaans, and deeply intelligent. We had met six years before, married and had babies in a few rapid years. Ruby was six and Jude just eighteen months younger than her.

I had written two books over that time as a magazine columnist and journalist, and he had been building his rising career in filmmaking, shooting commercials all over Africa.

The rafting trip had been to reconnect in nature after some gruelling years of parenting and spend some time in nature together.

The sun had scorched us both after a few days on the river and

It started with sex

we stood glaring at each other, faces red from anger and sunburn. I was almost as tall as him, and equally blonde. To outsiders we may have looked like two angry Amazon warriors ready to strike. Our hair was matted with sweat and mud, and our faces covered in dirt.

We were at war. It was a standoff.

Then he ran at me, picked me up and threw us both into river. Spluttering and choking we started to laugh. We lay in the shallows splashing each other. Both still furious, but willing to let it go.

He pinned me down and kissed me, laughing.

'Impressive,' I said. 'That you can still pick me up.'

'Strong, and smart,' he joked.

'And with rhythm!'

It was his 37th birthday a few weeks later and then life moved on and the fight, like so many, was packed away, unresolved and left hanging. So, the Easter holiday a few weeks later was pretty much doomed from the start.

We drove into the small east coast town of Kenton-on-Sea in the Eastern Cape on a storm cloud, with simmering resentment sharpening our words. Easter was celebrated with enthusiasm and when the kids were bundled off to their grandparents we settled in for a few days of fun. We ended up doing what most young, working, burned-out parents do when they have a few days off – we watched fourteen hours of a TV series back to back.

But on the Friday night we finally had a good time. We swam in the sea, went for a walk and drank some wine. I cooked fresh fish and we laughed.

Then we kissed. Man, it was sweet. The delicious kind of sweetness, when chemistry just works and you remember why you married in the first place.

Finally, all those months of tension and fights were forgotten. It was game on, and no small kids around.

Then we walked down the passage and tumbled into the bed in

the easy way we'd always had. It was always the simplest magic that brought us together.

We were hitting our groove. I was moving on top of him. Then he flipped me over and he was on top of me, kissing my neck, licking my skin and moving faster.

'Oh yes,' he was moaning.

Yeah baby.

'Oh God, oh God, oh God.'

Moaning.

Shouting.

No, screaming.

It ended in a strangled roar.

'Aaaaaaargggh!'

Then he collapsed on top of me. He was whimpering, and not in a good way.

I lay for a second, wondering what the hell had just happened. Had I just mistimed it all? Was he so excited to get it on that he had popped too soon?

'Llewelyn? What's going on?'

I shook him. Hard.

He was not responding.

I felt his warm body on top of me, his sweat mixing with mine, now cooling fast.

'Okay, enough. Come on! Stop it now. And get off me. You are really heavy and I can't breathe.'

He slumped lower and heavier on me.

I knew then he was unconscious.

My sweat turned instantly cold.

Getting out from under him was the first battle. I had a naked 110 kilogram man on top of me. I am no lightweight. I would be described as athletic at best, solid at worst. I am almost six foot tall. I did shotput and discus at high school. But he was a dead weight.

It started with sex

He was also wet with sweat and slippery all over. It was like a WWE match with The Undertaker just having landed on top of me. Except he was naked and there was nothing I could grab on to, to move him.

And I was scared. Heart-pounding scared.

What had just happened?

I rocked. I rolled. I pushed. Eventually I got traction and rolled him off me.

I scrambled out from under him, rolled of the bed and came up gasping. Finally, I could look at him.

His eyes were closed but I could see he wasn't unconscious. I knelt beside him.

'What is it? Tell me!' I was shaking him, shouting now. But he could not speak.

He contracted into a small ball, holding his head. I could see his body going into convulsions. I knew this was bad. This was not 'best sex of my life' bad; this was Big Bad. This was the worst kind of bad.

Now when things go wrong, I have two totally different responses. Inside me there may be a wild fear, but my voice and demeanour are calm and reassuring. I learnt this from running a busy newsroom full of junior journalists as news editor. You have to keep your cool. Some have even called it an underplay.

'Okay, let's regroup. Talk to me. How does it feel?' I used the Calm Voice.

Groaning.

'Speak to me!' I tried the Commanding Voice.

'Pain. Head,' he gasped.

Moaning.

'Okay (back to the Calm Voice), just focus on your breath. Slow it down. You are fine. I am right here next to you. But I need to know what is going on.'

He was gasping now. Desperate animal grunts.

LOVE AND ABOVE

'On a scale of one to ten, ten being a shark has taken your leg, how severe is the pain?'

No response.

Then finally. 'Sleep.'

No no no! Worst idea ever.

'Just want to sleep.'

Anyone who has the most basic medical training, of which I had none, knows that is not right. No sleeping, right?

'I am going to call your mom,' I threatened.

'Noooo,' he moaned.

I was reaching to call her, but I realised there was nothing she could do to help me from two hours away. I was alone in this. I was in a tiny seaside town . . . and I didn't even remember the name of the town in that moment. There were no neighbours. It was largely deserted and out of season.

'Call Murray,' he gasped.

Crap, even in his impaired state he came up with a better solution than me. Our doctor. His close friend. Just about the best person on the planet. Dr Murray Rushmere.

Get it together, Sarah, I chastised myself.

It was eleven at night. My hands were shaking so hard I could hardly find his number.

He answered immediately.

'Murray, something's really wrong with Llewelyn.'

I told his what had happened and described the symptoms.

'It doesn't sound good clinically, Sarah,' he said. 'Can you call an ambulance?'

'We are two hours from a hospital. I wonder if I can get him to the car . . .'

'Yes, try that first.'

I looked around the room for the first time.

I was still naked and I realised that the sweat had dried and I

It started with sex

was shaking with cold. It was April, and autumn, and the first step was logically to pull on some clothes. They were lying on the floor – a pair of shorts, a bikini and a summer top.

I looked at the bed, crumpled with our lovemaking. Curled up in the corner lay my big burly naked man.

On the floor lay his jeans where we had ripped them off earlier.

I eyed the jeans and sized him up. Could I get him dressed?

Nope, I would grab a blanket.

I stood above him and got my arms under his. At least that was the plan.

I couldn't budge him.

Right, honest assessment here . . . can I pick him up?

That's a big no.

What about a drag and drop manoeuvre? He was lying on the duvet and I could pull his entire body onto the floor and drag him on the blanket through the house and out to the car, which was parked in the driveway.

In fact, I could even get him onto the lawn and then drive the car right through the flower bed to the front door.

Fuck the garden and the new grass.

Yes! I had a plan now.

Shoes on. I start pulling the duvet.

Nothing. It didn't budge.

Practically speaking, I battle to hoist a 22 kilogram suitcase onto the scale when travelling, never mind carry it down the stairs.

And he was out cold.

Plan C.

'Wake up!' I screamed. 'Wake up. Get up!'

I shook him and slapped his face.

He groaned.

'Get up,' I ordered. 'I need you to STAND UP NOW.'

This was not going to work.

LOVE AND ABOVE

I called Dr Rushmere back.

'No way I can move him.'

'Is the pain getting worse?'

'No, it seems to be easing off,' I said. 'He actually seems to be coming round a bit more. He is more communicative.'

'That's a good sign. Okay. Look, I really think you should get him to a doctor. See if there is any way you can get him into the car. But check in with me in a bit. If the pain is getting better that's a good sign. If it's getting worse that's a bad sign and we need to get an ambulance to you.'

Oh Lord.

I didn't want it to get worse.

I didn't want to be left all alone in a holiday house to handle this situation, so I really wanted to get him to the car. Naked, clothed or anything in between.

I tried the Commanding Voice again.

'Get up!' I demanded. 'I am getting you to the car. Can you walk?'

This time he was more responsive, and he was forming coherent sentences.

'No. Leave me alone. I want to sleep.'

'Please just walk to the car with me. I will help you.'

I realised I was sobbing as the words came out.

I hauled him into a sitting position. It was useless. He pushed me off and flopped back down.

He went to sleep then.

I sat next to him the entire night, my body shaking with fear. Every few hours I woke him to check he was still conscious until I fell asleep, curled in a blanket on the bed next to him.

I opened my eyes and in seconds I was standing upright. I had fallen asleep in the middle of the vigil.

He was lying next to me, the blanket over both of us and his arm over his head.

It started with sex

He seemed to be breathing still.

'You alive?' I asked.

'Mmmmm,' he murmured and flopped his arm out to find me.

I limped to the kitchen, filled the kettle, brewed some strong coffee and sat on the stairs watching the sun rise as I sipped it.

The silence of the village felt eerie after the otherworldliness of the night before. Had that all just happened?

I waited until the sun had risen and it seemed respectable before I shook him awake. He was groggy and slow, but he got out of bed and showered.

'Talk to me. How do you feel?'

He shook me off.

'It's nothing. So much better.'

'You sure?'

'I have a bitch of a headache on one side, but not unmanageable and nothing like last night.'

'But it was extreme, and I am worried. I want to take you straight to the doctor today.'

'No, leave it. I am fine now and I will chat to Murray.'

I heard him on the phone, being ever so polite.

'I was making love with Sarah. I started to feel a tension, a fiery burn up the right side of my neck. Perhaps if I was watching TV at the time I would have paused and noticed sooner. But I was consumed with the moment, and otherwise occupied.

'I only realised what was happening when the pain exploded like petrol thrown onto a flickering fire. Suddenly this white-hot hand seemed to reach up out of my neck, gripping the right side of my head, squeezing my ear, my eye. It was like the worst kind of sinus pain I'd ever experienced and more. I fell down on the bed and all I could do was dive down into something like sleep where I felt I could escape the worst of it.'

They agreed to watch the progress of it and another doctor

friend concurred.

But I was scared. I had a deep feeling that this was not right.

I got the details of the closest hospital, which was in Port Elizabeth.

'I have an appointment for you for a CT scan,' I told him. He frowned and turned away, slow and clearly unsteady on his feet.

'Please leave me. I am not going.'

I called his mother and told her what had happened, leaving out some of the details.

'Ingrid, I am worried. I don't think it was just a migraine at all. But he is refusing to have it checked out.'

She agreed. 'See how he feels today.'

I insisted we drive to a small town nearby to visit some old friends who lived there. He wanted to stay home and sleep, but I wanted some backup.

I gave him some pain tablets and we set off. He was very subdued and quiet.

It was such a relief to be with others and not alone with him. As the day progressed, his headache subsided. They took over and made us tea and it felt like normality was slowly resuming.

Before lunch Llewelyn asked them if he could have a nap on their couch.

'Look, this isn't normal,' I whispered urgently. 'What can I do?'

'Let him sleep,' they urged. 'He's been under so much stress, with small kids and all his work. This is a massive stress release for him. A huge headache can happen as a way of releasing things.'

I wasn't so sure. The journalist in me wanted facts. The scientist in me knew a seizure was never a good thing and needed to be checked. My soul knew something was dead wrong. I knew it deeply, and in my bones. This was all wrong.

'I need a walk,' I told them. 'I am going to tour the town. Call me if he wakes.'

It started with sex

I walked straight the local doctor's office and spoke to them. I didn't have an appointment. but it was a small town and I insisted on a quick chat. They suggested he come in for a check-up. But they didn't have a CT scanner there, so the only option was the one two hours away.

When I got back, he was sitting in the sun and chatting to Murray, who was checking in on him. His iPhone was tight on his ear as he laughed. That phone had never left his ear for the past five years.

'I really don't want you to worry. I am feeling almost normal and when we get to Cape Town I will have a proper check-up,' he told me.

He had diagnosed himself as fine. So, we sat on the porch and drank tea and had a lazy Saturday with friends while we watched their kids. But when we were alone again at the holiday house that night, a sense of dread filled me.

I called his mom on the side and quietly shared my worry.

'I am worried too. Look, we are going to drive through tomorrow so we will be with you for two days. Let's both keep an eye on him.'

They came the next day with the kids and we cooked and swam, and the headache faded into the holiday memories.

I noticed he was taking a load of painkillers.

'It's still sore,' he admitted. 'But I told you, I will go for a check-up when we get home tomorrow.'

We drove home the next day as planned. He insisted on driving the entire way. All eight hours. He would not let me take the wheel once. I sat fuming, scared and resentful.

He was quiet. I was quiet.

The kids were listening to the Harry Potter audiobook in the back seat.

I had a deep sense of unease. I knew deep down that the train had left Platform 9¾. I didn't yet know just how fast it was all going to happen, but I knew that life was going to be very different.

The film director

We drove straight back to our home in Cape Town and into work and life.

He went straight back to his office and studio.

He had built a career as a commercials director on sheer talent, fast talking and a magnetic personality, and at 37 he was riding the wave. He was booked over the next few months to shoot several high-budget beer commercials in the Democratic Republic of the Congo, and he had a team behind him getting his vision realised.

I dived straight back into work, running a magazine publishing company I had built. In my twenties I'd been a financial journalist and then editor, and had moved slowly up the ranks from a cadet journalist covering the Asian derivative markets to working for a top political newspaper and then into radio. During all this I had written two books and had made a name for myself as an author. They were all about the trials and indignity of parenting and relationships.

After close to a decade as a financial and business journalist, at 34 I had built up a magazine publishing company on the side. It was small and quirky, and we had some great titles. One was the fun kulula.com in-flight magazine.

It was a great, profitable little business and it ran like clockwork, with me at the helm as publisher and the creative director Gary coming up with new and better ideas. We had offices just off buzzing Kloof Street in town, where my editorial team worked.

My books were selling well, and I had also started to run writing courses. That week, I had one planned. Eight authors were due to join me on a six-week novel plotting journey.

The film director

Ruby was six years old and at Camps Bay Preparatory School. Confident and outgoing, she loved school and made friends easily. She'd been born on the floor of our lounge one cold winter morning in a water birth, with a midwife ushering her in, when I was 28. I was making an investigative television documentary at the time about the high incidence of Caesarian sections in the private medical industry, and a home birth seemed like the right thing to do. Being a humour columnist, I'd written a book (my first) about the indignity of birth, the horrors of parenting and the battle to regain my waist. It was an unexpected hit.

Despite the crushing defeat of a child on our relationship we pushed on, and our second child, Jude, was born eighteen months later, on Valentine's Day. He also arrived in a birthing pool on our lounge floor – but that location was not by choice, but rather the unfortunate error of mistaking my labour for food poisoning.

At four he hated school and refused to go most days. I would end up taking him to the magazine office with me where he would happily play for most of the day. My second book was all about the demise of relationships after the kids arrive, aptly titled *Romance 101: How your relationship can survive your kids (and other passion killers).*

The epicentre of our family was Llewelyn. Blond, tall and powerful, he came from a proud Afrikaans clan and was he was simply Someone You Noticed.

As soon as we got back I tried to get him to go for a CT scan, but he had work demands and was feeling good.

'Just see a doctor,' I begged. But Dr Google had helped him, and he had diagnosed himself. This was the diagnosis: It was a spiritual awakening and part of a journey that he had been on for the past two years.

'I didn't want to tell you, but I have been having these strange moments of connecting for a while,' he told me over dinner after we had settled back in. 'It has happened a few times now. Mostly I feel so light-headed and I have to sit or lie down. But more than that, when it happens I feel as if the universe is opening to me. I can hear things, and smell things.'

I recalled them him calling me a few weeks ago, telling me about a strange episode. I had dismissed it at the time. So much was going on.

'Then about five weeks ago I was sitting in my office listening to a colleague when I suddenly become hyper-aware of everything happening around me. I could hear him talking to me. I was thinking about what he was saying, and it seemed at the same time I was also aware of everything else that was going on in the street outside, the room next door, and somewhere else that I knew wasn't as easily placed and explained as the room next door.'

I was listening then, and I realised that I had heard him say these things, possibly between toddler baths, tantrums, homework or story time. I hadn't really had time to listen to him closely.

'Except each time it happened it become more layered and nuanced. It felt like something, or some other time and place, was bleeding through into my waking awareness. At times it felt like a memory. At other times it felt like it was happening to me right then and there. Each time it was an aspect of the same thing. There were actually people in this other time or place I kept bumping up against, but I could never see a face or recognise anybody.''

'Do you think it is linked to your work with Colin?' I asked.

He nodded.

Colin Campbell was his coach, mentor and a renowned sangoma. For two years Llewelyn had been working with him as his client on a quest to connect more and more deeply with himself and his ancestors. Llewelyn had always done significant inner work, from spiritual development to personal growth, from meditation to psychology, and this was the latest evolution of his deep enquiry into the human condition.

I had consulted with Colin myself several times over the years. He

The film director

was gifted doctor of divination, a deeply intellectual and philosophical man, and was known as the master of throwing the bones.

'What's going on there, Llew? Why is this causing you to have these episodes?'

'As you know I went to Colin looking for something. It wasn't something that's easy to find. I just had this very strong feeling that there was something deeper I am meant to do in this world. Colin gave me a lot of things to do to help me to get connected with my ancestors, and I guess that has been building to this.'

I leaned back.

'So, this is a breakthrough? Do you think you are connecting with your ancestors in these episodes?'

He grinned, his eyes shining with excitement.

'I am not sure but for a while now I've felt like a new sense has switched on inside me. I felt like I was experiencing all this extra stuff on another level, in addition to the five senses we make do with every day.'

'Are you sure it is all supposed to happen like this? I mean, that was unexpected, right? Have you chatted to Colin about this?' I asked.

'Not yet because he's away, but I am going to see his brother soon.'

We consulted with our bigger circle of friends. They were alternative and open-minded. We were intellectual New Agers and fully exploring life, so when news of this episode spread they were thrilled.

'It's so amazing that he's tapping into his deeper intuition.'

'This is a massive healing crisis, something he has worked on for ages.'

'This is such a breakthrough.'

I was walking on eggshells between a deep sense of unease and faith.

I knew something was wrong. I had a deep, soulful intuition about it. I could smell it. Feel it. I had a thick, cloying feeling of dread.

LOVE AND ABOVE

And all I could feel was fear.

'It's not right,' I told my sister Liz. 'I'm not sure I'm buying this spiritual awakening. I mean, I'm totally open to all that, but it doesn't feel right.'

'I don't know . . . I mean, why would this happen otherwise? It sounds reasonable and he has been pushing so hard with his spiritual work,' Liz said.

Liz was my older sister by two years and had been my best friend for most of my life. She was shorter and smaller than me, and took after my father with his cornflower-blue eyes and gentle heart.

Two days after we got back, my concern was rising.

I had tucked the kids in and read them a story, and was lying in bed next to him. He had been tired and sluggish most of the day and I had noticed he was still popping headache tablets.

The house was quiet and dark, but I was watching him, sleeping soundly. As I lay there a dark presence did not let me sleep. I was rigid and alert, like a cat on a roof. When I tapped into my deep intuition, I knew that something was just not right.

I breathed deeply and let my mind expand and reach out, as I'd done as a teenager. I'd been deeply drawn to spirituality as a teen. I practised astral travelling, meditation and hypnotism. I devoured every book on past lives, karma and different religions. I explored channelling and Ouija boards. I would get messages and be able to hear voices, but more than that I simply had a sense of *knowing*. This knowing would range from clearly seeing that someone was ill, or that they had an injury or a wound, to being given a clear message for them. This sense had served me well in my life and as I got older and my explorations continued. I could turn it off or ignore it, or tap into it when I chose.

That night I felt something. I saw them, then. In the room above the bed there were spirits. Call them what you will – entities, spirits, beings – they were dark and circling. I lay frozen in fear.

Slowly I inched away from the bed. It was if there was an intruder

The film director

in the house and I was trying to slip out quietly. As I moved, I realised they didn't see me or track me. It was not me they were there for.

It was him.

Was it the shadowy light from the street outside? Was it my imagination? But I knew it wasn't. I knew I had an uncanny ability to see and hear things that others couldn't. It just wasn't always so visual.

But I wasn't going to try to unpack that then. I just wanted to get away. I tiptoed out of the room and stood at the door.

He lay asleep on the bed in a deep, heavy sleep. Above him I saw the dark masses circling.

I walked into the kitchen and turned on the lights. Normality. There it all was. The real world – kettle, tea and a warm golden light. I felt my hand fumble for the normal things, to do simple and human things like turn on the kettle, draw the tea and feel the warmth on my hand.

I slept on the couch that night. It was to be one of many such nights.

Relax, I told myself. Ever conscious of my own dark thoughts, and the fact I tend to expect the worst, I was fighting my instinct to catastrophise this situation.

But I also knew that something big was wrong. I even had a word for it, but I wasn't able to allow that word in yet.

I went back to work the next day. But I was like a cat that has sensed an intruder; I was just waiting.

That night I was opening the door of my office to welcome an excited group of writers. Eight novelists were joining me for an evening writing session and to work on their books. The kids were at home with a babysitter and I would be back late.

I was just setting up the room when my phone rang.

Caller: Llew the Magnificent, it read.

He had changed his name in my contacts again.

Last time it had been 'The smartest guy in all the world'.

LOVE AND ABOVE

'Grrruuuuurgh.'

A strangled voice came through.

'Come quickly,' he groaned.

My heart was in my throat. I had just put the kettle on, and my writing students were filing into the room and taking their seats. I snatched my bag and walked straight out the door. They were staring at me, waiting.

I didn't even explain. I was walking to my car. Running. I didn't lock the door. I didn't say a word. I just ran.

I knew. I knew. I had been waiting.

I kept him on the line.

'Where are you?'

'My office. On the floor. Head.'

The phone went dead.

I don't remember getting into my car or driving. I remember my hands shaking so much I couldn't get the key into the ignition. Then I was on the road and racing over the steep pass along the coastal road from Hout Bay to Camps Bay. His office was fourteen kilometres away. On a good day it would take 25 minutes.

I called my sister. Her film production office was a few blocks from his.

'Liz, I need your help. Llew is on the floor of his office. Get there please. Now.'

She didn't even ask why. She never did.

'On my way,' she said.

I broke every speed law on the winding road around the coast. I hit the number for Dr Rushmere. He answered on the first ring.

'He called me,' he said. 'I am already on my way to him.'

I was careening around the mountain pass, hazard lights on, my breath coming in desperate pants.

My sister called back. It had been an eternity.

'I got in. He is on the couch, and we are waiting for Murray. He

The film director

is . . . not good. He's in pain.'

Her voice was falsely cheerful. My family all tend to rally in a disaster, to calm the other person down. I could hear behind it a thread that was thin and scared.

When I pulled up in the loading bay ten minutes later, Murray was there, standing over the couch.

He looked concerned, his tall, lean frame bent over as he checked reflexes and temperature.

'I gave him an immediate shot of morphine, so he is groggy.'

'What's the hell's going on, Murray? 'I asked. The three of us discussed the options while Llewelyn lay dazed on the couch.

'It could be a migraine. We don't know yet and we need to run tests now,' he said.

'It's not a migraine.' I was emphatic. I knew it wasn't. 'I am taking him for a CT scan tomorrow.'

He nodded. 'It's time. I will send you a reference to book a slot.'

Llewelyn was woozy, but listening.

'To be honest, I have had a mild headache ever since our trip. If pressed I would admit that it was hanging around the right-hand side of my head. After a lifetime of no real headaches, I am now beginning to wonder what this is about.'

We got him home, between my sister and me. We manhandled him into the car and then out the car at my house again. We were both shaking from a combination of shock and strain. We somehow marched him up the stairs and into the house. We got him into the bed, and he went straight to sleep, without even changing.

I closed the door and turned off the lights, with a glance back to see if the dark mass was back above him. Not yet, but I knew it would loom later when the world stilled and went dark.

Liz helped me with the kids and we sent the babysitter off. When they'd gone to sleep we poured ourselves a large glass of wine and sat outside in the early evening, talking over the day.

LOVE AND ABOVE

I checked my text messages and there was one from the writing group. 'We are worried. Please let us know what happened,' it read.

Later, Liz left and drove back to her flat right on the beach, and the night moved on. I slept on the couch again, desperate for a bit of rest. I was so scared. My body was trembling with fear. I was sick with terror and the deep knowledge that this was bad news coming.

The next day I left him at home and went to work. I booked a CT scan at the hospital. The first slot was at about 4 pm.

'I will come with you,' I said.

'No need. I am happy to go alone. I am feeling so much better.'

'I am coming,' I said.

That afternoon I drove him to the Christiaan Barnard Memorial Hospital and we waited for the scan. He was shaken. I could tell because he was louder than usual. He made jokes and chatted to all the nurses, charming them and making them laugh. I was quiet and tense – a basket of nerves. He went in for the scan and I sat waiting and paged through the same magazine about eight times. I didn't read a word.

Finally, he came out and the nurse told us to go home.

'Your family doctor will call you with the results.'

I knew then it was bad.

He did not.

'Why?' he asked. 'Can't I get the results now?'

'Let's wait.' I pulled on his arm. 'Let's get you home.'

'No, I want to get the results.'

The nurse looked uncomfortable. I felt as if I was watching a slow-motion train crash, but I could not stop it.

She swallowed.

'Okay, then come through.'

She led us to the back office where the radiologist was sitting, shifting uncomfortably. On the screen in front of him was Llew's brain. In black and white. There was a quiet tension in the room and all the other radiologists turned away and were suddenly busy.

The film director

This was not our place, and it was not his job to deliver such news

'Let's just go,' I hissed. 'We can call in the morning.'

Llew was like a child marvelling at the screen, his photographer's brain looking at the light and images.

'Wow,' he said. 'This is incredible. Is that me? Is this the right hemisphere?'

He was fascinated with his own brain. But I could feel the nerves coming off the radiologist like nuclear blasts.

I knew what he wanted to say, as Llew was chattering on, asking a million questions, delaying the inevitable.

'Can I get a printout of this?' he asked. I stopped him then. My nerves were at the end.

'Quiet now.' I put my hand on his arm. 'The doctor wants to tell us something. Give him a chance.'

The man swallowed. He pointed to the scan.

'This is a lesion on your brain. It is sizable.' His pen circled it. 'Please call your doctor. He will explain it to you, and the next steps.'

We peered into the screen as if the swirling mass of dark and light meant anything to us.

'Thank you,' I smiled firmly. *What a ridiculous thing to say,* I thought as I walked out. I wanted to say, 'Fuck you,' at the very least . . . 'Shut up and take it back.'

Instead, I walked out to pay.

I led him out with me. He was quieter now. Before we'd left the reception area, he was on the phone to Murray, who was on speed dial.

'Murray. They tell me I have a lesion on my brain,' he said, his voice booming across reception. 'What does that mean?'

There was a long pause. A very long one. He was on speakerphone, and I leaned in. We were standing in the foyer now, waiting for the lift.

'That means you have a brain tumour, my friend. It is not good news.'

LOVE AND ABOVE

Murray always spoke the truth. It was delivered in the simplest language. There was no other way to say it.

He knew that only the truth was enough.

I texted Liz.

It's a lesion.

Tumour.

I drove home that night, a tight, quiet unit of unease. But with the unease came a strange feeling of relief. We had a word for it. He had a brain tumour.

The sangoma journey

Tracking.

That was the word for the piles of tiny brown notebooks by his bed. He was tracking himself. This was one of the tasks set by the sangoma teacher he had been studying with for close on three years now. His cellphone alarm went off every twenty minutes and no matter what he was doing, he would stop, slip his pen and notebook out of his pocket, and note the time and what he was doing.

Tracking himself. It was part of the rigorous self-examination he was so willing to do.

There were other things that had started and grown during the process. One was eating no sugar for over a year. Another was cold showers only. For the entire winter he had only allowed himself to shower in ice-cold water. But more confusing ones had emerged, and things were feeling uncertain.

He was on a spiritual quest, and it had started out simply a few years before, but it was getting more and more intense and complicated. This current journey was into fatherhood and how he could more fully be a man in the world. He was working to be present and engaged with his family, and on a deeper quest for his life path.

As I walked in the next morning, eyes hollow with pain, he was noting down his movements. He snapped the tracking book closed, his movements slower than usual.

Nothing about Llewelyn was slow. Not his mind, not his speech and not his person. He was the smartest and fastest person in any room. And often the sexiest too.

'I am getting the kids off to school and then we have an

appointment with the neurologist,' I told him as a I put a cup of tea next to his bed. His face looked thick and slow.

'What time is the appointment?' he asked, sipping the tea.

'Eleven, so I will come and fetch you just before. I need to go into the office and just sort a few things out.'

Normal.

That's what we would do. We would be normal.

We would not mention that there was a big growing mass in his head, nor that his parents were already looking for flights to come to Cape Town that day. I would not tell him that I had been busy the night before, placing those calls for support early.

I had been up early and got the kids moving. Ruby, a tiny terror of a blonde dictator, was already dressed and having breakfast. Jude was naked in the cold winter morning. Getting him dressed would end in tears most days.

I was so grateful for the normal bustle of the house, the sounds of the kitchen as chairs scraped and cereal bowls chinked.

I sat down next to Llewelyn and he grimaced up at me.

'Sore?' I asked.

He nodded, clicked his pen, noted something in the tracking notebook and slipped it back into his pocket.

That tracking had been annoying me a lot lately. It had started off interesting and had become obsessive. It interrupted everything. The cellphone alarm would go off and whether we were talking, eating, driving or walking he would take out that notebook and write down his thoughts.

His bedside table was not the tangled mess of technology it usually was. By this time in the morning, he would have his headphones on and be listening to a talk on his phone, he would be making calls and issuing orders.

'I want to come with you.'

He threw back the warm duvet and stood up and I saw him bend

The sangoma journey

over in pain and dizziness. I lunged towards him and steered him back towards the bed.

'Just sit down,' I told him, guiding him down.

Tall and solid, his blond hair tousled from sleep, he sat back, confused. He shook his head as if clearing it.

'Did I imagine yesterday?'

I shook my head.

I crouched down in front of him and took both of his hands. I kissed the top of his head and breathed in the smell of him. It was musky and male. I buried my face in his hair and then pulled him close.

'Let's just take it slowly, okay?'

He nodded.

'I'm going to take a shower and come with you.'

'On the school lift?'

'If that's okay. I will come with you and then come to your office. I don't want to be alone,' he said.

My heart sank.

I knew I had a full day in my diary at the office. I had a big contract I was trying to sign off.

None of it mattered.

'Of course, get dressed.' I faltered. 'Or do you need help?'

He shook his head.

In the car, the chatter with the kids was light and easy. It cut through the dread that spread in the front seat.

His alarm went off as he slipped out his tracking notebook, took out his pen and uncapped it, about to write. Then I saw his hand shake.

He put the cap back on and put it away. I put my hand on his leg.

'Let's get you into class,' I trilled later, my voice thin with artifice as I scooped the kids out the car one by one and dropped them off at their classrooms.

Silently the two of us drove the snaking road up from Camps Bay and over Kloof Nek into the City Bowl. He leaned back against the seat and closed his eyes.

My office was in a small side street, and I parked, and we both walked over to get a coffee from the little shop around the corner. I heard his tracking alarm, but he simply turned it off.

'Decaf?' I asked. He shook his head.

His headache from two days before seemed to be gone. His blue eyes were shining and clear again, and he took my hand as we walked back to my office.

I was the first one there, as I was the boss. I unlocked the door and disarmed. I knew that in an hour a few journalists would walk in, drop their laptops and head for coffee.

We stood in the sun in small garden for a moment, taking a few sips.

'Shit, babe,' he said.

'Shit,' I echoed.

'You worried?' he asked me.

Worried?

The word 'worry' seemed so small to express what I felt. A deep, clawing dread. A fatalistic knowledge that everything was about to go to a ball of shit. That everything I knew as good was over. A raging sea of terror that wanted to pull me in, but that I was holding back with artifice and bravado.

No, I wanted to scream. I am not worried. I am absolutely terrified.

But instead, I nodded.

'I am. You?'

He grinned, his eyes shining with the pure excitement of a small child.

'Hell, no. Something crazy is happening to me and I think it is the breakthrough I have been looking for,' he said.

He had been telling me that 'something' had been happening for a while. He had called me a few times over the past weeks, euphoric,

The sangoma journey

from shooting a commercial in the Congo.

'I am connecting. It is as if a veil is lifting between me and the other worlds,' he told me. 'I am starting to hear voices, smell things. This is what I have been working towards, this connection.'

He had been doing some strange things, and was getting particularly vehement about this spiritual practice.

Mystic experience – or seizure?

Llewelyn's diary: Travels in hyperreality
If you like me haven't been hanging out in hospitals, then you will also be wondering what on earth a 'lesion' might be. As it turns out it's not 100 well-drilled Roman soldiers. It turns out that it's doctor-speak for a tumour.

This was the first moment that the word 'tumour' had popped into my head, and no sooner had it landed I promptly put it down again. It has a real hot-potato-like quality. It radiates a tangible energy.

I've never suffered from headaches. The only painful head pain I've ever experienced was during several dental operations to remove my wisdom teeth during puberty. That was technically not head pain, but in my jaw. But like anybody who's been 'hurt' by a dentist, it feels even more intense because it's so close to your brain.

I remember wondering at the time if an amputated toe hurt as much. If somehow the nerve impulses could somehow lose some of their urgency if they travelled over a greater distance. Anyway, the question was obviously not important enough to answer because I didn't go on to study medicine and neurology. Instead I chose to become a student and practitioner of a different kind of signalling science, filmmaking. I chose to explore and learn how to send signals through the air, using the power of light to flicker and touch a different set of nerves, to trigger a different set of impulses.

When Sarah and I were alone that Thursday evening when I got the news I had a 'lesion' I felt, dare I say, excited. There was no part of me that thought that this would end in tears. This feels like the first time I went overseas, sitting on the plane, flying to America age eighteen, exhilarated to be sailing into the unknown, so hungry for what was going to happen next.

There has always been that part of me that, like a meerkat, sticks its head out of the burrow at the first sign of anything vaguely interesting and out of the

Mystic experience – or seizure?

ordinary, even if it is burrowing inside my head.

Thursday night I slept, if that's what you can call it. I woke up exhausted. It felt like I had spent the whole night pouring the left part of my brain into the right and back again.

Friday was a busy day, full of distractions, things to do, people to meet, places to go. It was the day of the general elections. Murray booked me to see a highly regarded neurosurgeon, Dr Grant White, and the plan was to see him with the CT scan from Thursday and let him guide us from there.

From ship to shore, from pilot to guide.

Dr White had me check myself into the Cape Town Mediclinic where I met him later that morning. He popped up to see me on one of his tea breaks, between brain operations. The moment he walked in the door I felt good about what was happening.

He asked me if I had been experiencing any 'other symptoms'. And this is when my world started to crash.

I let him in on what to date has been a very personal journey and for me in no way connected with what was going on . . . or so I thought.

I told him about my increasing awakening and the 'new senses' that had been switched on.

I confessed that this week at lunch I had an experience that I later described as a 'low blood sugar' moment. I was sitting in a coffee shop when I suddenly felt like I might faint. I was with a filmmaker and friend when I slid off the chair and lay on the slate floor wondering what was going to happen next. I asked her to get me something with sugar. The juice arrived and five minutes later I felt that I wasn't going to faint after all, climbed back on my chair, seemingly normal.

If you keep reading you will soon begin to regard this word 'normal' with some suspicion. I suspect you may come to realise, if you haven't already, that normal has got very little to do with anything interesting and life-affirming.

Back at my office later that day I was seeing a client out and when I got back to my office I had another one of these 'blood sugar' moments, only this time it was much scarier. I was losing consciousness. I had visions of passing out and nobody being able to get to me so I leopard-crawled to my office door – which latches from

LOVE AND ABOVE

the inside – and made sure the latch was off. That was when I scrambled for my cellphone and called Sarah and then Murray, my doctor, and with some urgency asked him to get to me as quick as he could.

It was at this point that Dr White, my neurosurgeon, nodded.

'Those are seizures.'

What could I say?

At that point it dawned on me how limiting the maps are that we have drawn up to describe the territory we find ourselves in.

The doctor's map tells him I'm having a seizure.

My map tells me I'm experiencing a world beyond my borders.

Of course there was nothing else to say to Dr White at that time. Probably because he sent me to the Christiaan Barnard Memorial Hospital where I had an MRI scan, lying inside a narrow sarcophagus that huffs and puffs with a myriad of magnetic pulses and impulses. A friend wrote to me later about her experience of hearing 'God' talking to her during her MRI scan and I knew exactly what she meant.

En route back to the Cape Town Mediclinic I had another one of my mystic experiences (or seizures) and was very relieved to be back in the hospital. I was attached to a drip and put on to an anti-seizure medication.

Dr White appeared later in the afternoon to tell me what his prognosis was.

I had an 'aggressive' tumour behind my right eye which had to be surgically removed as soon as possible.

I went to sleep on Friday night at the clinic, drugged up to the eyeballs and talk of brain surgery that still left me feeling excited and a more than a little intrigued by what this all held in store.

Prepare for brain removal

When the neurosurgeon had come in to deliver the news he'd brought a nurse with him, and I noticed she had a syringe primed on a tray with what I presumed was a tranquilliser.

'Brain cancer.' 'Aggressive.' 'Stage 4.'

'How sure are you?' I asked.

'Ninety-eight per cent. We know the presentation of this particular tumour very well from the scans. It is a typical one.'

He turned to Llewelyn.

'We are going to schedule surgery for next week so you will have a few days at home to get ready. We also want the swelling and bleeding to go down first.'

He nodded.

'Doctor, do you think my mobile phone caused this?'

For the past few years, his phone had never been far from his head. His Nokia and then his iPhone. Years back he had cancelled his Telkom contract and sworn only ever to use his cellphone. He could spend hours on the phone and ran his entire business off it.

It was the source of many fights between us, not only because of the health hazards but also the social annoyance of having someone always on the phone.

'Just a week ago I was on a work call for over an hour and I noticed my entire phone was hot against my head.'

'The tumour is in exactly the place on his head where the phone sits,' I added.

Dr White shrugged.

'We can't be sure what causes these things. It is possible, but we cannot pinpoint the cause. We are keeping you overnight for observation,' Dr White said sternly to both of us. 'We want to watch you and keep you on the drip, but chances are you can go home in the morning.'

I had almost buckled at the knees with relief. Someone else was going to look after him for a night.

'Thank you,' I said. As if he hadn't just delivered what is possibly the worst news anyone can deliver.

He walked over to Llew and put his hand on his shoulder.

'Get your affairs in order before the surgery,' he said.

'You mean his will?' I asked.

The nurse looked at me.

'No, I mean get the hospital pre-approval done. But, yes, I would also recommend you get all that sort of paperwork done. That is always advisable.'

The nurse holding the syringe and clipboard backed out of the room and we discussed logistics and when I would collect him.

'You will not be allowed to drive for the next two years, and I am going to suggest that you never drive again.'

With that resounding warning he left us alone in the room.

I turned to the nurse who was following him out.

'Are you going to use that?' I said, pointing at the syringe primed with tranquilliser. 'Can I get that shot?'

I left him in the ward and climbed into my car and drove in a daze to collect the kids from school. I called my office and told them I wouldn't be back that day and to lock up when they left.

I knew Llewelyn's parents were already on their way to Cape Town from their home in East London, and would arrive that night to stay with friends. They didn't know the diagnosis yet, but his mom would know what to do. Ingrid always knew what to do. Someone would know what to do to fix this, wouldn't they? Help was on its way.

After dropping off the kids and making them lunch, I called

Prepare for brain removal

the girls. My tightest and closest girlfriends, Lulu and Georgia, and I formed a circle of three. We call ourselves the Triumvirate.

'It's worst-case scenario,' I told them.

'I am coming over tonight with some meds for you,' Lulu said. 'You need to be calm.'

'Send me the details of the diagnosis,' Georgia said. 'I want to send it to a friend to check it out.'

I went to see Liz, driving to her office down the road in the leafy suburb of Tamboerskloof. She had bought the offices a few years earlier to house her growing business and they were in full production mode that day. Cape Town was one of the most glamorous and versatile places to shoot films and commercials, and she had built a solid business in that field. She was in the middle of an international commercials shoot and the courtyard was full of trucks, lighting and crew. She stood in the middle of it with her long hair tied up and a tired look in her eye. She saw me coming and rushed over.

She listened quietly as I filled her in.

'How is this possible?' she asked.

There was no answer.

We walked into her office, full of mad production crew and gear.

'Sarah, I have to tell you that I chatted to Nicky and sent her the scans. She told me some bad news, that people never survive this. She said that he may have six months, maximum two years, but there is no hope.'

I stared at her and shook my head. Nicky was a radiologist.

'I'm sure that's not what he has got. They don't know yet what it really even is.'

She nodded.

'Let's call some people and pull in the troops to help,' she said. 'You are going to need a lot of support to get through this.'

Phakalane Centre for Ritual

We had a few days to prepare for brain surgery and the house filled up with friends and family showing support. Ingrid and John had arrived. I was not alone, and Ingrid stepped in fast.

'I am going away for two days.' Llewelyn came out of the bedroom on the second day home with his bags packed. He was in his jeans and trainers, and his hair was tousled and messy, but his eyes were shiny and clear.

'Where you going, Daddy?' Ruby asked, running to him and holding him tight.

'I am going to do a few days of silence at a retreat centre. I need to be quiet for a while and think.'

I dropped him there later that day. As we drove, we didn't speak much.

We hadn't told the children what was going on yet. We were keeping it from them, but we knew we had to tell them very soon. We had to tell them something. We were both clear that we would not tell them about the cancer. Cancer was such a big word, and they were so small they would not understand it. We would frame it in relatable ways.

'Shall I tell the kids what's going on while you are away?'

He shook his head. 'No let's wait until I come back. I want to tell them.'

'They know stuff is going on. Your parents have arrived and there is a total flurry of people. Also, it's hard to keep conversations away from them. We have to tell them soon. If they ask, I am not going to lie to them. I will tell them you are going to have an operation soon, right?'

Phakalane Centre for Ritual

We agreed that was a reasonable story.

'Have you got your phone?' I asked.

He shook his head.

'I don't want it near me. I left it at home, so you won't be able to get hold of me. Can you collect me on Sunday when I am ready?'

'Are you going to be alone at Phakalane?' I asked.

He shook his head. 'Claudia is there and we will work together.'

Claudia Rauber was waiting to greet us as we drove into the gates of the magnificent centre. I felt a sense of calm. Another person who knew what they were doing was on the team. She stood over six foot tall with the lean and wiry body of a panther. She had built, and ran, this spectacular world-class ritual centre in the forest of Hout Bay with clean German precision and total dedication. She was a friend to both of us, a teacher and a sangoma.

She was also quite scary.

Without a word she took the bags out of the car, hugged me tight and smiled. She was wearing her hiya. She would later be the second sangoma at the ceremony where the chickens were sacrificed.

This centre she ran was deeply familiar to both of us. This place, and these people. We had spent many hours here doing ceremonies, rituals, dances and events. We were alternative and wacky and interested in exploring life in all its realms.

'Can I walk around for a bit? I will let myself out,' I asked.

She nodded and took Llewelyn's arm, and firmly steered him inside. They walked up the steps and into the building and the door closed.

I turned to the huge and sprawling indigenous garden that stretched up the mountainside. I knew where I was going. Hidden between the trees and behind a huge pine was a clearing, a circle of emptiness in the lush and rich garden.

It was here, just a year ago, that I had knelt on the ground before doing a sweat lodge. It was late at night, under the stars. We had been

LOVE AND ABOVE

holding a sweat lodge in the Native American style. This was very different from a traditional African steam. It was hotter, and longer.

The lodge was being run by Claudia, in all her shamanic glory, and attended by a group of powerful women I knew well. All of us had done work together before on the spiritual journeys we had been on during our thirties.

That night we had entered the lodge with hot rocks and prayer bundles.

I had done many of these lodges a few years before when I had apprenticed with Native American elder John TwoBirds. I had joined his Neo-Traditional tribe and started to learn the ways. I had learnt how to prepare the low lodge for the ceremony, how to make prayer bundles and to tend the fire with hot rocks that would be passed into the hut.

It was just a year before that we had been there, and that night the songs had come back to me easily and sweetly.

Louder and louder.

Faster and faster.

Hotter and hotter.

We sang and prayed and drummed as our voices rose over the suburban houses around this magnificent place as more and more hot rocks were passed into the lodge. The heat was so intense and the songs so loud.

It was only hours later when we crawled out of the lodge and into the open cool night air that I noticed something was wrong.

I wasn't in my body. I was above it. I was higher in the sky, closer to the tree line.

I was on the floor shaking and convulsing. I was watching, from above, this naked woman on the floor. Me. Scared now.

Liz was one of the women who had been in the lodge, and she noticed first. Then they crowded around me. I kept watching from above.

'I. Am. Not. Okay,' I managed to gasp. It had been so right inside the lodge, I had left myself lift off, soar. But outside it didn't seem right. It was terrifying and I didn't know how to get back.

All that night I battled. The others went to bed, and I lay shuddering and convulsing on a couch. They covered me with blankets, massaged my feet, made me eat something solid (which I promptly threw up) and then got me in to a hot bath. Eventually, exhausted, Claudia went to bed and I was left with Liz, who curled up behind me on the couch and held me all night.

And so here I was. Back a year later and kneeling on that same ground.

That night my prayers had been for me. Now they were for him.

That night came flooding back to me. It hadn't ended the next day. It had continued. As the easy light of the sun rose, I was still soaring.

A part of me was in my body – the Sarah who was lying on the couch, sipping tea. I could function. I could talk and get dressed. But another part of me was still soaring up in the sky. Further away now. Harder to reach.

I was still convulsing and shuddering. Liz got me home and put me to bed. Days later I was still vacant. Llewelyn was carrying on as normal and handling the children as I lay still. We told people I was sick.

People came and went, and I moved like a zombie though the house. My friend Georgia took me to a psychiatrist who told me I had dissociated and gave me Urbanol. I went to a psychologist who told me it was a trauma response. I went to a massage therapist to rub my feet and ground me. I called a friend who did energy work and she tried to help.

My mom came over got me up and into the sun. We went for a walk and I counted every step. One. Two. Three. Four. I got to 500.

It had been a week since the lodge and I was still not okay.

Finally, Llewelyn suggested we call Colin and describe what had happened.

'Has this happened to you before?'

'Not since I was a child,' I said. 'Not for decades.'

'But you know this feeling?'

I nodded. I did.

'Yes, I know this. I used to practise astral travelling as a teenager. I was very interested and got quite far. But this is the next level. I am not even sure what is going on. I am just not here, and at the same time I was out there in the skies.'

'Hmm. It seems that part of your sprit has not re-integrated yet.'

'Can you fix this?' I asked.

'It will all come right, just give it time. You will find your way back. Focus on your body. Go for a walk in the sun. Count each step. Drink warm things and eat grounding foods.'

'Is that all I can do?' I was desperate. Desperate to be normal. Desperate for this to end. 'Can't I come see you? You can help me.'

'Only time will help. Take off all your clothes and lie on the grass. Face your head north and spread your arms out wide. Lie in the sun for ten minutes each day.'

'Day?' I echoed. 'How long could this last? Please, Colin, I need this to end. I just want to be normal. I want to be able to work and look after the kids.'

'It will end when it is ready. But things will start to improve each day,' he told me.

I put down the call and stripped off all my clothes and walked naked outside, to the only small patch of grass we had that ran next to the swimming pool.

'What you doing there?' Llewelyn called to me.

He was sitting on the deck having lunch with a table full of guests. He had ridden the Argus cycle tour that morning with his mates. They had all come back to our house for a lunch.

The conversation stopped.

Phakalane Centre for Ritual

I looked at them and walked over to the grass and lay down, face to the earth. I spread my arms and buried my face in the patchy soil and let the sun warm my back.

The table resumed its chatter – looking back, I'm sure it was very nervous chatter – and I felt a small warm body lie down next to me. Ruby had padded over and lain down beside me on the grass.

Now I was back in that same clearing where that lodge had taken place, a full year later. I knelt in the middle of it, closed my eyes and let my hand dig into the ground. I was less crazy, now, but no less willing to connect to the elemental energies of this world. This time, someone else was in deep and urgent need.

I knelt low and said a prayer. I said it to the soil, and then whispered it to the wind in the trees.

'Save him.'

Fear: I know you well, old friend

What do you do when you get the news that someone you love has a *tumour*? In their brain? I mean, could it not just have been an aneurysm?

After leaving the clearing I drove to my parents' house, careening over the mountain towards it. I climbed into bed and stayed there for two days. I was beyond all words.

Fear. I know you so well. You are back.

I first met you when I was eighteen. It was a heady summer as we graduated from school and the world was ahead of us. University was calling, and our futures were so bright. A week later my friend Eva was shot dead in a botched hijacking. The girl we all loved. Gone.

Everything changed after that, and a visitor arrived. Fear. Worry. Anxiety. Depression. All aspects of the same feeling that life is somehow going to go wrong, and you have no control over it.

These visitors followed me to university and all through my twenties. At times I could push them away. I drank them away. I talked them away. I went to psychologists to get rid of them. I medicated them away. I danced them away. I worked them away.

Fear. Nothing will push this away.

My mouth is dry. Dry as a bone. I cannot even swallow for the dry taste on my tongue. I want to run away from the news, from the radiologist, from the neurosurgeon, from the thoughts.

'It's not you who is sick,' I keep telling myself. 'It's not you who should be in fear, shock.'

My mind is dragging me down. Down into the thoughts that are unthinkable. Thoughts that are not rational.

The fear train has left the station and it is gathering speed.

Fear: I know you well, old friend

I want it to stop but all I can do right now is feel.

Feel the pain. Feel the fear. Block it out. Get through it.

When I crawled back out of the bed two days later, I showered and had a cup of tea. I called the kids, who were staying with their ouma, and made sure everyone had been looked after. I checked in at my office and signed off a magazine that was ready to go to print.

I tidied the room, thanked my devastated parents.

Then I put my armour back on and went back into battle like a warrior.

A missing piece of brain

Llewelyn's diary: Travels in hyperreality

I arrived home exactly one week after having the tumour removed from my brain.

Before I'd left the hospital I had a visit from my neurosurgeon, Dr White, and then a day or two later from the oncologist to discuss first the histology and then the proposed treatment.

The histology showed what they had expected, a malignant tumour, which he was able to remove in its entirety.

'However, the tumour is like a beehive,' he explained. 'You can see the beehive and remove it, but you don't know how many bees are outside of the hive at any given time.'

These 'bees', of course, being other cancerous cells in the surrounding tissues, possibly reproducing and making more cancer cells. 'So the focus now,' Dr White explained, 'is to kill any remaining cancer cells.'

Enter the oncologist who explained that for this particular type of brain cancer there was a 'best practice' used worldwide and I was on it.

Six weeks of radiation combined with an oral chemo drug.

The chemotherapy will be pills. I was given a long treatment: six weeks of chemo, followed by a three-week holiday. An MRI scan to see how I've responded. Then I will keep going with the chemo and have a scan every six months.

So that was that sorted, then?

This morning my heart is heavier than I expected. It is suddenly leaning under the unimagined weight of what my family may be feeling or thinking right now.

A strange new reality meets me around every corner. I was and still am overwhelmed by an overwhelming feeling of feeling.

I have wondered if, by divine intervention, the neurosurgeon removed that part of my brain which has been holding the reins of my waking hours for the last 38

A missing piece of brain

years with such cunning control, allowing me only rare glimpses of what it might be like to feel too deeply.

Last night I spent a few hours on a medical brain tumour website.

The website was very caught up in a patient's survival rate and provided some very neat statistics of how many cancer patients survive how many days from their diagnosis. It went according to age, kind of brain tumour and a whole load of other factors. I am sure there is a huge amount of energy that goes into giving (or attempting to give) people something that looks like certainty in what is ultimately a completely uncertain time.

The numbers tell me I may be live between two years and ten.

How do I feel now?

Now that I've seen the kinds of numbers for what I have – a stage 4 astrocytoma.

That I may not make it to 40?

I now had a sense of why some people were so alarmed at my news.

Until last night it never once occurred to me to ask, 'How long have I got?'

How incredible to be faced with that question. The last time I thought this was lying on the floor of my house, hog-tied with five burglars ransacking my house.

The other question in my mind is, why me?

Of all the people who live unconscious lives, people who smoke and drink. Why me?

I feel as if there is somehow an expectation and a belief that if we do certain things, behave in a certain way, we will be spared in some way.

That has been ripped away.

Maybe inside me there is a guy who isn't taking this prognosis of an aggressive form of brain cancer so well. Who isn't deeply excited by this challenge, and this adventure. In fact, he is taking this all quite badly.

What may he, this guy, be feeling?

He may be scared to suddenly look at his life, which stretched open in front of him until a few weeks ago. He may be terrified that instead of the horizon he now sees an approaching 'event horizon' with a big red bus on it that is heading straight for him.

My magazine goes bust

It was only two weeks since the Dirty Easter Weekend and we were in a fight for life, a medical emergency.

The 'normal world' was gone. That cosy and comfortable world we had lived in had simply been wiped out. The golden couple – a young family with a house, two cars and wildly creative careers – was vaporised. Obliterated. Suddenly, we were living in a totally different world. Even the air felt different. Food tasted different. Things sounded different.

This was the world of fear and terror.

It was the world of prayer.

It was the world of shock.

It was the world of friends rallying round.

It was the world of MRIs and brain surgery, of ICU and sleeping on the floor of the hospital.

I was just trying to get through every day and keep the kids and my business on an even keel. Visitors were pouring in. Teachers had to be informed. Everyone wanted constant updates.

At the very same time, in the very same week as he was discharged, I got an email that I had to pitch to keep my biggest publishing contract. This contract was a long-term one and was the financial bedrock of my company. Basically, it kept my company afloat.

The email was succinct. 'We are relooking our contracts and suppliers. Your publishing contact is up for renewal, and we would like a re-pitch.'

In shock, I was still trying to keep it together and appear vaguely normal. I flew to Johannesburg and went to the meeting to re-pitch the

My magazine goes bust

work. I was up and back in a day.

I don't remember a word I said in that meeting, or a single moment of that trip. The next week, the email came.

> Dear supplier
> Thanks for four years of a great relationship. Unfortunately, we have decided not to renew our contract with your publishing firm and have decided to go with another publisher.
> Warm regards
> New Marketing Manager

It was years later when I learnt that this other publisher had been courting the client for some time. The contract was over with one month's notice. I had to inform my joint venture partners and our entire sales team was suddenly out of jobs.

Without that contract, I knew my publishing company could barely survive.

I could have saved it. I could have rallied and got more clients, pitched on more magazines. But I could not have cared less about all the things I had thought so important before. The world was a different place.

Navigating conspiracy and cancer

Llewelyn's diary: Travels in hyperreality
It took me almost a week at home before I dared to go online in search of more info.

There was a part of me that didn't want to get too familiar with how the doctors saw me or my condition. I can appreciate how useful the labels are for them in helping them navigate what must be a very difficult landscape. I say 'difficult' because I did start to research and find out more about cancer in general and brain cancer in particular.

The more I read, I started to wonder how a person who becomes an oncologist to 'heal' people with cancer must function with such a limited toolset of radiation and chemo. They have a very chequered history and jury's still out on whether they actually heal.

Little did I know that I was about to uncover one of the biggest unanswered questions of our modern age.

The questions seem to be, in no particular order:
- *What really goes on in Area 51?*
- *What happens when you die?*
- *What causes cancer and how do you heal it?*

One of the first distinctions I discovered was that the combination of surgery, radiation and chemotherapy does not technically heal the body of cancer as much as it removes the tumour. To heal the body of cancer something else often needs to happen, something that addresses the underlying cause, what gave rise to the cancer in the first place. But nobody can agree on what causes cancer! So where does that leave us, where does that leave me?

All the reading left me feeling between a rock and a very hard place. On the one hand I had great doctors prescribing six weeks of radiation and chemotherapy

Navigating conspiracy and cancer

and on the other I had an avalanche of 'alternative therapies', all vying for pole position. Not only did the alternative therapies demand their moment in the sun, their advocates also spent a huge amount of energy painting the 'Big 3' (surgery, radiation and chemo) as an evil triumvirate cooked up by a cabal comprising the American Food and Drug Administration (FDA) and 'Big Pharma', intent on keeping their monopoly on 'approved' cancer treatments that they can profit from and squashing any treatment that they couldn't own even if it did show promise or even heal people.

So how did I navigate this?

Intellectually I couldn't resolve this. It was a minefield, with both sides taking great pains to paint the other side negatively. What really set my alarm bells ringing was noticing how much energy was going into making it a black-and-white issue. So, I took the third way. I felt my way through it, is what I did.

Ironically the harder part of the journey now is to navigate the myriad of alternative therapies. It seems there are enough alternative therapies to suit every kind of personality, eye colour and taste.

How do I feel?

I felt a real discomfort and sense that I did not want to be where I was for the first time.

I acknowledge that perhaps it is time to admit I am feeling a bit scared. Now, as I sit here, on the eve of the next big phase of this journey where I start radiation and all my alternative therapies, I feel ready.

If I wanted a walk in the park, I'd be in the park.

Greeting the ancestors

He was home, with staples in his head sealing up the cut in his skull and a huge question mark that ran across the entire shaved surface from his ear to his neck.

Being a photographer, he was thrilled with the sci-fi visuals and immediately got a friend and fellow photographer to shoot it. He put it on Instagram and mailed the image to everyone, with a huge question mark over his skull and the line, 'What seems to be the question Mr Roderick?'

And so two parallel healing journeys began.

One was in the halls of the oncology ward, where he was measured and fitted for a radiation mask. This was the start of the process that was going to keep him alive for as long as possible. The treatment plan, we were assured, was the 'gold standard' in treatment for 'his type of cancer'. The radiation mask was made a week before the therapy started. We met the team that would treat him for the six weeks in the radiology department, as well as the team that would handle the chemotherapy.

'These are some of the best people I've met in a long time,' he told me as we drove. 'I feel that I can go far with these people. I could feel that they care and that they are committed to me healing. That has decided it for me.'

He was equally exuberant about the other healing journey.

This second journey was taking place in a far wilder place. This may have been the middle-class suburbs of Tamboerskloof and Kalk Bay, but it was beyond the tangible.

His first request once he got home was that I take him to see the

Greeting the ancestors

sangoma Niall Campbell, Colin's brother. It was as if a secret door had opened and revealed a world just behind this one. The gatekeeper of this world was Niall.

'You need to meet Niall formally,' Llewelyn told me after a few weeks. 'I am going to study with him".'

I'd met Niall. He had been to gatherings I had attended. He carried a real power and I was both scared and delighted by it. I was drawn to him, and intimidated by him. He was different from anybody else I had ever met. I wasn't sure I wanted him to come to dinner.

Niall and Colin Campbell were brothers and worked together often, but in different ways. They are Batswana by birth and Scottish by descent. But both are deeply African, respected by the local communities and keepers of a custom many black Africans themselves have moved away from.

I'd heard they had recently spent several weeks traveling in the remote Altai Mountains, consulting with indigenous elders in relation to eco-mapping work and traditional shamanic knowledge.

I'd watched a documentary on them a few years before and knew that their work had taken them to ancestral homelands and forgotten wilderness, from the Amazon Basin to New York City, the sacred sites of Venda and remote Ethiopia to Russia. I knew Niall had been photographed for an exhibition called White Sangomas by world-renowned artist Pieter Hugo.

He worked with clients from all over the world, who travelled all the way to Africa just to see him and work with him. Many years before, he was known as a doctor of initiation up in the bush of Botswana, taking people through the gruelling sangoma training and initiation process of twasa.

'But where's Colin?' I asked. 'Why aren't you sticking with him?'

'He's living in the UK, lecturing and teaching at the Schumacher College on Deep Ecology for a while, but he's out for a visit so he will come for dinner too. I want them both to come over so you can meet them. I will be working with Niall a lot now and you need to understand what is going on.'

When they joined us for dinner, we sat in the garden and chatted over a light meal. Both kids joined us, taken by these two very interesting guests who towered over us at well over six foot four.

Ruby was an inquisitive and interested child, and she was particularly drawn to the two lofty and strange guests. She sat at the table asked lots of questions.

'What's a sangoma?' she wanted to know, directing her question at Niall and listening closely to his unusual accent.

'Well, people use that word a lot now, for many things. But the word "sangoma" actually means the People of the Song – or the drum, or the ceremony. When we get a little bit deeper, a sangoma is somebody who works with the ancestors.

'People come to us if they have troubles; sometimes they want us to throw the bones so that we can see why they have trouble and some people come because they are looking for a different way of living.'

His voice ran like music over us in the early evening light, and we sat entranced.

'How did you become one?'

He smiled and leaned back. 'To become one, you have to be called. The call often comes in the form of dreams or visions. Or other times you may get physical or psychological illness like depression. But the call cannot be ignored.

'Being a sangoma runs in families. In my family we are all sangomas. Colin and my sister Heather are both sangomas. My grandmother Gilly was quite a famous healer in the Catholic faith. She used to pray for people and put her hands on them if they were sick. She also used to brew up a whole lot of different kinds of magic oils and powders that she used to help people. My mom told me that my grandmother's grandmother was also a healer and did the same thing.'

Jude sidled up. 'Dad says sangomas can talk to dead people.'

Greeting the ancestors

He nodded, giving the small blonde inquisitor a studied answer. His voice was low and deep, and his accent was at times confusing.

'We can. We talk to them to tell them things, to ask them things, and sometimes just because we want to talk. We call this pahla. But we don't just speak to dead people, we speak to many people who have come before us who we see as important.'

I leaned in close. 'Can they talk back?' I asked.

He shook his head.

'Not always. I think our ancestors can hear us. I think they see us and watch over us. I think it's just hard for us to hear them because they don't have the same kind of bodies that we do. So, when they talk, it's really hard for us to hear, and also it's really hard for us to see them. It's like trying to see air. But like air, we know they are there even though we can't see them or hear them.'

He smiled.

'But we can talk to them. That is what prayer is. We can tell them things and I think they like that. I think they like to hear how we are, just like when they still had bodies like us. Sometimes we even offer them things like water, tobacco or wine.'

Llewelyn was quiet that night as he listened. He wasn't his usual exuberant self and I felt something was brewing.

We could have sat all night listening to Niall talk, but the evening ran late and it was time to get the kids into bed and ready for school the next day. That night my mind was racing, poring over the strange and wonderous ideas that had been shared in our garden.

I wasn't to know yet how many nights I would spend talking with Niall, or how deeply I would listen to his voice in the years to come.

The bika ceremony

A ceremony was to take place at our house and a special announcement was to be made.

Llewelyn was recovering from surgery and was gaining in strength as his radiation started, but more time was spent in sessions with Niall.

I was given a list of food to prepare and dishes to make. There was a list of important people to invite and it was specified that it had to be in front of the fireplace. Luckily we had one, even though it smoked badly, and I rushed to get a chimney sweep.

Dr Murray and his family.
Ingrid and John – Llewelyn's parents.
Kath, his sister, and her then-husband.
My mother and father.
Liz and Jayne, my two sisters.

When everyone had arrived, we all put our hiyas over our shoulders and waists as the ceremony began.

Niall had brought some of his lodge of sangomas to support him, and he spoke to us all.

'In our Western world, we have a certain way of approaching illness. Our first question is, can it be cured? In my world, the first question is often, why do I have this sickness and how does it work? As if knowing why and how will affect the outcome. We ask: How do I accommodate it?

'When Llewelyn first came to see me, he told me he had a bad headache. When I threw my bones, I saw a lot of different things in them. One of the things I saw was that his life was about to change completely – the bones showed a sign of calamity. The other thing

The bika ceremony

I saw was that he was being called. But it wasn't clear then what the calling was about.

'As you know, he had been working with Colin for a while and my brother gave him things to do and things to think about. That's how sangomas often help people – they give them ways to open their hearts so that the things that are hiding in the deep, deep parts can come up. Then we can see these things and think about them and let them show us how to live.

'I didn't see him for a very long time after that, but I heard what had happened. When he came back to see me, he looked like Frankenstein with all the metal stitches in his head.'

The room was still, everyone listening closely.

'But when he sat down in front of me, he looked excited. The first thing he said to me when he sat down was this: Why did I bring this into my life? This is the question we often ask as sangomas.

'He told me he was interested in exploring this calling. We don't yet know what the calling is, but what has emerged is that he isn't going to twasa and become a sangoma, but he needs to do what we call men's work.'

Llewelyn stepped to the font of the room, stood next to him, and faced us all.

'We are here today to announce that Path to you, and to his ancestors. He has a path to follow, and he has to follow it fully.'

He placed a hat on Llewelyn's head made of jackal skin. This was the traditional hat of a koma doctor.

'The path is like walking through a canyon – you can't divert from the path. You can't go left or right. You can't negotiate with it. You are all invited here to know this, and to keep him on this path. To show your support for this.'

Then Niall put two bangles on him, one made of copper and the other of brass.

When he had finished, we all knelt in front of the fireplace and the pahla began. We bowed our heads low and clapped. Tobacco was offered and placed on the floor. Beer and whisky were offered to the ancestors and poured for them. There were four cloths in a bowl, which were offerings to the different ancestors.

Niall's voice rose in our lounge and twisted with the fire and was carried out into the air as he spoke in a lyrical and rhythmic prayer. After every line he spoke, we clapped. All together. All white, yet this African way was so easy and instinctive. Next to me knelt Ruby and Jude, shrouded in their cloths and totally entranced with the ritual and ceremony.

Both of Llewelyn's parents were game, and we were all excited by this new addition to our world. They were both Christian but open-minded, artistic and cool. They let their children lead, and they supported what they did with grace and a few giggles at times.

When we had ended, we celebrated with ululating and cheers. Then we sat down to a feast and laid two places for the ancestors.

Murray had known Niall and his work for many years and had worked with him and invited him to teach and lecture on herbal medicine, so this world was easy and familiar to him. Murray was not just any doctor but a calm and centred man, deeply spiritual, and interested in exploring the meaning behind disease and holistic paths to healing.

This was new to all of us and the ceremony and the structure of it seemed exciting, and important. It felt more solid and supporting than the meetings in hospital consulting rooms or in radiation waiting rooms.

Later that day, when all the food had been cleared and the house was quiet, we sat on the couch and chatted. The kids had friends playing and it was school the next day.

Neither of us had worked for a while and I was feeling increasingly stressed by that. I wanted to talk about it, and our plans. He was distant and preoccupied.

The bika ceremony

'Can we talk about it another time?' he asked.

He had radiation the next day again. It was making him tired; his head was painful and the skin tender.

He had carefully taken his jackal hat off and placed it in a special bag with all the magical items he was gathering. He sat next to me, turning his bangles around and around.

'What are the bangles for?' I asked.

'They are a sign of my commitment to this path, like my wedding ring, and mean I have agreed to this path. I cannot take them off.'

Gathering the drums and throwing the bones

'Mom! Dad has a dead genet in the garden we are skinning it. Come look, it smells *so bad.*'

Jude rushed up to the door as I walked in. His blue eyes shone with excitement. The estate agent was standing behind me, coming to evaluate the property. Over the previous few months we had moved out of our rental house and bought a house in the quieter coastal suburb of Hout Bay.

'Is your husband a taxidermist?' the agent asked, eyebrows raised as Jude dragged us out into the garden and the rank smell hit us.

'Erm. Yes, an amateur one,' I said.

There was indeed a dissection taking place at the outside entertainment area. A sheet of plastic covered my new balau outdoor table and on it was a dead wild cat being delicately parted from its fur. The kids' blonde heads were bent over the task, along with Niall and Llewelyn.

'We also have a porcupine in the freezer,' Ruby told the agent, looking up from her task. 'Mom found it on the road for dad on the way to school, so we collected it in a plastic bag for him. We also have a frozen civet. Dad is going to make the genet into a pouch to hold the bones.'

Her eyes were her father's – cobalt blue and questioning under her shock of curly blonde hair. The two of them looked like a unit as they bent back over the animal. Niall had not looked up, the sharp knife slicing the skin away from flesh slowly and methodically.

We had also built a traditional prayer room (a ndumba) in our

Gathering the drums and throwing the bones

garden. It was packed with all sorts of herbs, exotic animals, bones and skins – and the door was kept firmly locked most of the time.

The house evaluation came back low.

A few months had passed and our lives had settled into an unorthodox routine.

Once a week he went for radiation sessions, and then it was on to his chemo regime.

He also started a trail of alternative treatments. Every well-meaning friend had a 'sure cure for cancer'. Trips to an iridologist, ozone therapy, acupuncture, aura photography. He drank peroxide, had vitamin C drips, and used Bemer blankets and a Rife machine. We did alkaline, paleo, keto and vegan diets – all at different times. Buckets of turmeric were stocked. We bought a juicer and did a green juice regime. We started doing Transcendental Meditation again twice a day, and he started having cold showers again.

There was no alternative treatment stone that was left unturned.

Llewelyn approached his healing and shamanic training the same way he approached his life – he was all in. He never did anything half-heartedly. Whether it was an eating plan, a job or an opinion, he was totally committed. And so he was dedicated, committed and focused on curing himself.

Over time, one extra modality that stuck was Chinese medicine. The herbs had to be cooked and boiled for hours before the water was stored in glass jars. Our kitchen had the permanent rich smell of brewing mushrooms and wild roots, and he would drink the concoctions multiple times a day.

Amid the smells of skinned animals and wild roots, we did all the normal things that a suburban middle-class family would do. The kids were at school, and this dominated life. It was a daily rush of school sports, gym and parties.

We had given them some of the information, and they understood that a growth had been taken out of Llewelyn's head and that he was healing. And so life resumed.

Ruby, ever so perceptive at age six, took me aside one day, looked into my eyes and asked, 'Mom, I need to know this. Could Dad have died from the tumour in his head?'

I nodded. Her eyes widened with shock and fear.

'Can he still die from it?'

'He can, my Binks. If it comes back, he can die. But we don't think he will.'

She shook her head.

'Don't tell Jude?' she asked me. 'He's too young.'

Then, 'Mom, promise me if it comes back and he is going to die you will tell me.'

'I promise you,' I said.

As Llewelyn focused on his healing journey, I took over all aspects of the kids and house. We also had a huge and close circle of friends who all wanted to help. His circle was wide and vast. Mine was equally so. Between us, we were a power couple.

My primary support was my sisters, my mom and the Triumvirate. There were queues of people wanting to drive Llewelyn around, and simply visit and chat to him. Our house was an endless social gathering of events, parties and visits.

I was getting back on my feet and writing for international magazines to bring in some income. I turned my attention to researching all the alternative treatments for cancer. Not satisfied with anecdotal stories of 'a friend of a friend who cured themselves' or 'spontaneous remission', I would track down the actual person and try and verify it, or call doctors and scientists. I used the basic mantra of journalism – verify, check and confirm. Very often, the story of healing was loose and unsubstantiated.

A spontaneous remission? But first they most often had surgery.

A green diet? Yes, but also chemo.

An acidic body? Not medically possible.

Gathering the drums and throwing the bones

As I had lost my company I was still in free fall, and for the first time in my working life I wasn't working endlessly long hours. As part of his diagnosis, we had got a payout from our dread disease cover and were living off that money. We had taken most of the payout, added our savings, and bought this house. We were stretching what was left of the lump sum as best we could.

The sangoma's dance

'We are dancing on Sunday. Do you want to come with me?'

'What, like 5Rhythms?' I asked Llewelyn.

My younger sister Jayne was a dance teacher and was training to be a facilitator of this dance form designed by Gabrielle Roth, so we often joined her in these events she organised. The crowd we were in, and my siblings, were all Alternative with a capital A. We dabbled in all these things that open the heart and make you feel different – ecstatic dance, yoga, Nia, 5Rhythms, Biodanza, sweat lodges and ceremonies.

I had done so many of these modalities and practices over the years in some relentless pursuit for personal growth, and had gathered a tribe around me that was equally open-minded and open-hearted.

We had dabbled in these things, but we hadn't lived that life. This was all about to change.

'No, it is formal sangoma dance,' he said. 'It is something very different to anything you have seen before. But I am assisting and my lodge is hosting it. There are sangomas coming from all over the country, and it is an honour to be invited.'

'In like Flynn,' I said, not even sure why I felt so excited.

That Saturday we drove to a magnificent property in the green forests just on the edge of Hout Bay. I heard the sound of drums from the street as we arrived. The stage was set and it was electric.

There was a German man in his sixties, a top consultant in her forties, and a schoolteacher. There were black and white and all races gathered. In all, there were about 30 people there and we all headed down to the dance area, a sandy clearing in the trees where the drums were being warmed up and prepared.

The sangoma's dance

We are familiar with social dancing. Ritual dancing is different. Dancing in this way has been used for centuries as a way of accessing other worlds and in the African tradition it is the way in which each sangoma allows their spirit family to visit and descend into their body.

Each sangoma has their own song, their own steps and their own dance. It is not them entirely who dances, but the spirits they live with. In another world it could be called possession. But the container for it feels ancient and safe. It comes from a place before churches and labels and the world of law suggested that a close connection with the world of spirits was a bad thing.

I asked lots of questions of the gathered guests about what was going to happen.

Roxanne was a hairstylist, American and in her late twenties. She walked with me, explaining what was going on.

'A dance is a time we seek for a communication with the ancestors,' she told me. 'We don't dance often, but we should at least twice a year. It is the time when we allow the spirits we work with to come and visit us, and to inhabit our bodies for a short while.'

We were lugging mats and cloths down to the circle.

'How long have you been a sangoma?' I asked her.

'In my twenties I was diagnosed with severe mental health issues, but I didn't accept this and I knew there were other things going on that were beyond the realm of a medical diagnosis. Even though I was American I knew I was being called to another path and that my life had to change. I spent months with Niall in the bush doing my twasa. This is how I learnt to manage and control the voices and the experiences.'

Niall joined us, carrying a huge drum down the hill towards the circle. He joined the conversation.

'When you have struggled with a sickness or a calling of the ancestors there are signs. Things happen. Things get in the way of your life. It means that somehow you have started to accommodate an ancestor.'

LOVE AND ABOVE

'But how do you know if you have a calling?' I asked.

Some people battle with mental health. Some people have seizures, intense dreams, or health issues. Other times you can find things, get signs or messages.'

'How did you know you were being called?' I asked.

'That is a long story for another time, but I had several petit mal seizures and mental blank spaces between ages ten and twelve. I lived on a farm, and I was being attacked by animals. My father was an anthropologist and took me to see the Basarwa (San) tribe during one of his trips into the remote bush. They did a healing trance dance and when they came out of the trance they told me what it was.'

'So how does this all link to the dancing?' I asked

'When an ancestor wants to visit your body, it can feel like you are going mad. Sometimes it is called a personality crisis and it may feel like your personality is being overlaid by other personalities.

'One of the things we do during training is learn to differentiate these other voices from our own. Then we learn how to allow them only to be present at one time. You learn to gain control of them. Dancing is the place where ancestors are warmly invited to actually come into the body – but only at that specific time and during that specific dance.'

The day was moving and the sun rising higher as the preparations continued.

Llewelyn was the apprentice, the junior of the lodge, so he was doing all the heavy lifting. He was sweeping the dancing circle, carrying drums and making sure that all the visiting sangomas from further afield were looked after. There was a strong chain of hierarchy and place here, and at the top of the chain was Niall and Colin Campbell.

Niall was the 'father' and was addressed as such – 'baba'.

After what seemed like hours of preparation, we were ready to start.

It had been explained to me that each sangoma would wear a

The sangoma's dance

specifically designed traditional outfit that had been carefully made over time. It is the same outfit every time. When the sangoma puts it on, it is a signal to the spirit to come.

'It also means the spirit shouldn't come when you don't have that outfit on,' Niall had explained. 'When the spirit comes it has a lot of energy, so we work with that, and we allow it to dance and sing. There is a very rigid ritual at these dances with a lot of respect and formality.'

I was gripped with excitement and sat right in the centre of the action, at the edge of the circle, draped in my hiyas. I now had my own ones that I kept in my own cupboard along with the ones for the kids, as we used them so frequently.

The excitement mounted and the first sangoma was preparing to dance.

Four big drums started with a fast pace.

I shot into the air.

It was as if someone had passed an electric current through my body and I was on my feet in a second.

My heart was racing and my entire being was alive and activated.

I stared around, amazed. Nobody else seemed to feel this, everyone else was smiling and starting to clap.

'Sit with me.' Roxy motioned to me and waved me over.

I shook my head.

Calm down, I told myself. But I couldn't. The beat of the drums sent something through my body that was creating a shift in me. It was as if my entire being was vibrating with an energy and my soul was rising to it. It was literally rising, as if I was going to float away over the trees.

I knew this feeling. My mind raced back to that sweat lodge just a few years before. The feeling was the same. I was lifting off and I didn't want that to happen again.

I didn't even grab my stuff, I just turned and raced away from the circle, up the twisted garden path and to higher ground, closer to the safety of the house. Still the rhythmic beat of the drum was calling me and heating my blood.

Not far enough away.

I raced to the house and went inside and closed the door. A television was on and it provided a feeling of safe normality.

Safe.

I was safe from the call of the drums and the strangely wild things that happened to me when they started up.

That entire day I stayed inside, the muffled sounds just touching my ears. By later afternoon I ventured back outside, closer to the dance. I watched from afar, scared to go back in the space where the drums were calling me to something else. I wanted to stay on the edges of it.

Each sangoma took their time to dress. Each one's ritual garb was garish and dramatic. Huge horns and bangles, animal skins cut into headdresses. One had a walking stick and a pipe. Another a madly woven Viking dress.

The day built to the final dances, which the elders danced. Colin and then Niall. Then it was over. Llewelyn was not to dance that day, as he was still apprenticing and the dancing was one of the things you learnt over years.

Food was served and I watched as Llewelyn packed up the kit along with the other lodge juniors.

Niall came to sit with me for a bit, cooling his hands off in the pool. There were thick blisters from the hours of drumming he had done.

'Why does the sangoma who is dancing keep asking for different songs?' I asked.

'There are many different kinds of songs, and they have different kinds of drumbeats. The drumbeats are called nations. If the beat comes from the Zulu nation it's one kind of drumbeat, if it comes from Ngoni nation or the Xhosa nation it's another kind of a drumbeat. It depends on the origin of the spirit and how it wants to dance. They

The sangoma's dance

want a song that is theirs – even if it's a Northern European song or an old Afrikaans one.'

Things were getting deeper and stranger and more exciting. I climbed back into the car that night with a million thoughts in my head.

'I feel as if you may have fallen down the shamanic rabbit hole and I am right next to you in it,' I said to Llewelyn a few nights later as he was packing a bag for another trip to Botswana.

'Well, I sure have, but you don't have to come with me,' he said

'But it seems like I do. I am being drawn closer and closer. I am worried that I am going to be sucked in too deeply. You know how hard I have worked to ground myself.'

I eyed him as he carefully folded his cloths and packed the bones he was gathering and learning to throw. Snuff and oils then went into the suitcase. There was barely any room left for clothes.

Usually, he would have spent days packing and sorting his camera gear and technology – phones and cables and about every new tech you could find.

I stared at him for a long time, not entirely sure I knew him.

'Llew,' I said, 'do you feel you have changed since the surgery?'

He frowned.

'Do you?'

I nodded.

'You are very different now. I almost feel as if your personality is different and that the man I know so well is hard to reach.'

I ran my fingers through his hair. It was dark and curly, no longer the short, blond, cropped cut I loved, but a lanky, long style. A beard covered his chin.

'You even look different. Sure, your hair is different, but you also have changed more fundamentally. I am not sure if it is your path or the surgery.'

I ran my fingers across his skull, where a big dent sat from the surgery.

LOVE AND ABOVE

He had another MRI due the next day, before he left later in the week. His radiation had ended and he was only on the oral chemo tablets, and the ongoing Chinese herbs. The day before an MRI was always fraught for both of us.

'What do you mean?'

'I know this path is your choice, but it is taking you further and further away from me, and the kids. I feel as if I don't know you at all sometimes, like you are a stranger.'

He frowned.

'Sarah, you know this is what I have to do. I committed and we all agreed.' He twisted his metal bracelets around and around on his wrists, like small anchors holding his course. 'This is what I have to do now.'

I nodded.

But he was different. No longer the edgy and powerful man. No longer so insightful and sharp that he would pick up every nuance. He was gentle and emotional. He was vulnerable and soft.

It was frankly disturbing.

'Well, let's just get through tomorrow's scan and then take it one step at a time. I do need to find work and that is going to be my mission in these weeks you are away.'

He got another clean scan and we all breathed a sigh of relief.

The Naked Man medicine

Llewelyn flew to Botswana to the Campbell farm to run a workshop there, and was due to be away for at least three weeks.

This workshop was for the Gaia Foundation, on African Cosmology and Natural Law. It was part of the bigger work Colin and Niall were doing to decolonise and highlight the greater wisdom of indigenous approaches to life, community and the land.

This work was challenging the western myth of development and the model of pursuing money and progress at all costs. It was suggesting that older, traditional cultures were not 'backward', but actually contain many of the answers to questions about successful living, strong community, health, meaning and identity.

Indigenous communities maintained a set of systems that enabled them to live for millennia in harmony with nature. This does not mean these communities were free of warfare, human pettiness or even crime. But they sustained their lives and developed their cultures without destroying the natural capital on which they depended.

Part of this work was taking decision-makers on a deep immersion in the bush and the wild to give them an understanding that nature has laws. It was also to show them what indigenous communities do to maintain harmony and to ask how to move our present system towards greater balance. This generated Niall's professional income, along with consulting sessions and being paid for rituals and results.

That week, people from Kenya and Ethiopia, Ghana and Venda, England, Sweden and America were due to attend the workshop in Botswana.

Niall, Colin and Llewelyn had flown up a week early to prepare everything. But first they had a ceremony to do. Colin had built a new ndumba on the family farm and they needed to 'seat the ancestors' and say pahlas on the place. This was important so that Colin's ancestors would know what the ndumba was and that they were welcome there.

The week brought good news, which was delivered to me in a series of calls over a few days that broke up due to the bad connection on the farm. Llewelyn had found his medicine, and there was much jubilation at that event up north.

I had started a morning job running a photographic studio and a weekend job running a jewellery stall at a design and food market.

Between my two jobs and the school lifts and I pieced together the story.

It had unfolded over two days. The Campbell brothers had invited their teacher, Gogo Tshwene, to the important ceremony that opened Colin's ndumba.

'Gogo Tshwene was Niall's teacher's teacher,' Llew told me over the breaking line. 'She's a tiny little old lady with tiny feet and a very loud and high voice and she is a very senior sangoma. When she arrived it was a great honour, and we had to greet her in a special way with a lot of noise and drums. We had to bring the ancestors the way we do at a dance.'

Niall took up the story. They were both narrating on speakerphone.

'When we finished, we couldn't find Llewelyn. We looked everywhere and finally we heard a little sound coming from behind the ndumba. He was sitting all huddled up and crying. When we asked him, "Llewelyn, what's wrong?", he just cried and was shaking all over.

'Gogo Tshwene looked at him and started talking to him in her language, slowly, gently, kindly, she spoke and spoke. Finally, he told us he had seen a lot of people all around and that they were calling him. Then Gogo Tshwene told us that the ancestors had come to him and that he was being called to be a healer. When we told him what she said, he started shaking and crying all over again, but he was so happy.'

The Naked Man medicine

At that point the phone connection broke off and I had to wait a few more days for the rest of the story.

I was standing on the edge of a soccer field watching Ruby's first practice when the phone rang. Ruby was a talented singer and musician, but not a natural athlete, so she was nervous and kept glancing at me on the sidelines for reassurance. I walked to the side of the field and sat on the grass to listen to the strange story coming in instalments out of the bush.

Llewelyn's voice was far away, and it echoed the emotional distance that had grown between us. He was so excited to tell me the rest of the story.

'The night Gogo Tshwene left I had a very strange dream. It was so vivid and clear. I dreamed of a stream, with water lilies in it and green grass on the sides, and then I looked up and saw a green man on the hillside next to the stream. He was calling to me and waving me over. I told Niall the next day, and he said he knew that place but also that I was describing a medicine plant that he knew very well.'

'We all got in the truck and drove there. We parked next to the stream, and then we walked a bit. I saw it immediately, the spot on the hillside where the naked man had been standing calling me.'

I was totally gripped by the saga as the soccer match began. The noise was climbing as parents started to shout and cheer. I moved further away, waving at Ruby so she could see I was still watching.

'Niall took out his snuff and we started to pahla to the ancestors. We said thanks for the dream, and thanks for what the dream meant. We said thanks for everything that had happened the day before, and thanks that we were in such a beautiful place.

'Then Niall told me that the plant I dreamed of is a very powerful medicine. It called me to this place in the night and I had to find it. I was getting very excited, Sarah – I tell you, it was all so clear to me. So I got up and crossed the stream, climbed up the hillside and went up on to the rocks where there are trees, slowly, just following my heart.

LOVE AND ABOVE

Then I saw it.'

'What was it?"' I asked, pressing the phone closer to my ear as his voice started to break up. I walked, trying to find a better spot.

'A plant,' he said, his voice high with excitement. 'At the base of the tree in among the rocks, there it was. A light-green plant. The round green part sits on the ground and out of it grow long creeping tendrils that climb up trees. The Naked Man.'

'What?' I shouted. 'I can't hear you properly.'

'Sarah, I found it. Marotobalo – the Naked Man. It was crazy and Niall told me that it is very rare. It's not easy to find even if you have lived in the bush all your life.'

'But what is it?' I asked, glaring at an overenthusiastic father who was screaming next to me.

'Marotobalo is apparently a very rare and special medicine.'

But the volume of the match was rising, and it was difficult to talk. Ruby kept glancing at me, checking if I was watching her, so I cut the call short.

'Sounds incredible. Tell me more later, okay? I am watching Ruby in her first soccer match!'

I could hear the disappointment in his voice. This was a big deal for him, and I wanted to share the excitement, but I was simply worlds away from a green plant that was going to change his future. I was in the world of trying to pay the bills and care for two small children.

I turned back to the field and snapped my phone away and waved at Ruby.

Later, I would fetch Jude from a playdate at a friend and start the nightly ritual of feeding, bathing and settling the kids alone. I wondered if I would call him back once the house was tidy and the kids asleep to get the end of the story.

Probably not.

Wild rapture

It is closing in on three in the morning and sleep is the furthest thing from my mind.

I am in Botswana again. This is the third trip I have taken up here in the two years in which we've been on these parallel treatment and healing journeys. Life is slowly returning to a level of relative normality. The well-wishers have tailed off, MRIs are less terrifying and have all come back clear, and the work in Venda and Botswana is heating up.

Llewelyn is now very firmly on the path to becoming a koma doctor – a doctor of rites. In order to do this, he need to get through a ritual for men's rites of passage quite quickly and then start learning the work of these rites.

We had a celebration of this news, and a dinner to mark the occasion.

Niall had started initiating a group of men with him, including Llewelyn's best friend Richard, and much of the time is spent doing ritual steams (sebololo). They are working with an ancestral practice called 'washing the air', which is getting somebody 'straight with their ancestors and straight with their lineages'. At the same time, Llewelyn is learning medicine and herbs.

Some of these events happened in Venda, and others in Botswana, where I am tonight.

In February each year we'd have a 'first fruits' ceremony, which is when we'd eat certain things from the fields, with all the living and all the dead.

The night is electric as the relentless call of drums stretches out into the air under the African stars. In front of me dances an old

LOVE AND ABOVE

African man, Thembitongo – his back is bent, his eyes half-closed as his feet tap out an ancient rhythm. He is old and in pain. It is hard and painful to watch him as he creeps along in a shuffle-dance. As he falls to his knees the drums stop their call.

Thembitongo calls to his ancestors for blessings. His prayers are received by the watching crowd with claps of appreciation and a resounding 'makhosi' (thanks) in an age-old ritual that will play out all night.

Then his Xhosa greetings stop and he switches to a language I am far more familiar with: American. Thembitongo is not actually Xhosa – he is American. Nor is he old. He is 27 and grew up in Portland.

Two years ago, Thembi was called Doug. He studied mechanical engineering at the University of North Carolina. He is white and upper-middle class. He now lives in a rural village in the Transkei, where he is training to be a traditional African doctor and spirit channel.

Doug is part of a growing community of younger people looking for greater meaning in life. Many of them are turning to indigenous cultures to find a deeper connection to the world they live in. Because there are so few indigenous cultures left in the world, a lot of them have come here, to Africa.

There are even more guests this year than before.

Ya'Acov Darling Khan is an urban shaman who lives in Devon and takes people on dance workshops as part of his growing School for Movement Medicine. Mpateleni Makaule is princess from Venda who runs a foundation that is working to revive traditional culture and practices. Londoner Liz Hoskins is the head of the Gaia Foundation. Baba Ndimande is a ritual doctor living in a backwater town, but she travels the world as far and wide as Germany, Saudi Arabia and Turkey, working with clients.

There are heated conversations in the hot African bush. Over lunch we talk about a growing flood of westerners who are coming to

Wild rapture

find answers for life in traditional cultures. Niall believes that the soul is searching for older ways that are more in tune with the earth.

'People the world over are seeking alternatives to the North Atlantic paradigm,' he says. This is the model of work, spend and produce. Most of us live in cities and we work from the age of eighteen, most of the day. Most of us never actually ever touch the soil with our feet. We never take off our shoes until we go to bed and then it's a carpet or a tile.

'We are totally out of touch with nature and with the cycles of life. We work to buy things, to accumulate and to spend.

'We are kept busy working and we are told not to look inside ourselves. It is conditioning that makes us think this is normal. I don't think it's normal and the end result is that there is a disconnection between the things that keep us connected with each other, and with nature.'

Another guest in the wide-open land tonight is Henry Fletcher. He too feels that disconnect. He too has been called to discover a deeper relationship with the earth.

He met Colin at a Reclaiming Wildness event in Hampstead.

'I thought it was a costume party and so I spent hours making a tribal mask out of wood I nicked off a friend's tree,' he tells me. 'But it wasn't a party like that.'

The group met in a small flat in south London over tea.

'We sat in the lounge on couches in a circle and each person talked. We did a sharing circle about the loss of wildness in our lives. After the discussion we all split up for quiet time alone Everyone sat on a cushion for twenty minutes in meditation before we came back and shared our personal reflections,' he tells me.

Earlier tonight we crawled together into a traditional African steaming hut under the open skies. Before we entered the hut, we danced around and around in a circle under the full moon in the middle of the African bush to the drums and the screams and calls from our

LOVE AND ABOVE

own voices.

Then we got on our knees and entered the steam tent set up next to the fire. We chanted and sang as the pace got faster and faster. Hot rocks were passed into the tiny hut as herbs and song carried our voices higher and higher.

Herbs were put on the fire.

Herbs for joy and beauty and luck.

When the songs ended it could have been hours, or days, later. It was timeless. Then it was time for each of us to crawl out of the baking hot steaming hut. We were splashed with ice water and stood, some naked and some in sarongs, spluttering under the ancient stars.

'This is totally wild,' Henry smiles.

I feel it.

Wild.

This is wild without drugs or clubs. Without a thumping bass and a cracking hangover.

This is a wild rapture, found under ancient skies and on ancient land.

And when you feel it, and connect with it, you feel as if you are touching the heavens. I am here, in the rapture and the magic.

After the steam we dance some more. There is no talking circle. There is no silent sitting. There is no lounge with tea served. There is no quiet time. It feels like there is no civilisation, even.

And still the drums beat on into the night and we dance.

'You have to sing,' Niall tells me. 'You sing to connect to the divine or spirit. We call it going into air. Air is the etheric connection with the other realms. We get there by using song.'

Doug/Thembitongo comes to sit next to me later and we both nurse some tea. He tells me he found Niall through a dream he had one night in Portland.

'I was living a pretty regular life. I was sleeping next to my girlfriend and I had a really vivid dream. The dream was incredibly

Wild rapture

powerful and in it I was told three very clear things. I had to leave the relationship I was in, move to South Africa and contact someone called Colin Campbell.'

As luck would have it, Campbell was not hard to find. He was in California at the time presenting a talk at an inter-spiritual conference. He told Doug to get hold of Niall, rather, in Cape Town.

'I had another dream, that of a man wearing white beads on his forehead – the beads of the Xhosa tribe living in the Transkei. When I told Niall the dream, he knew what to do.'

It was there that he found his spiritual teacher and decided to undergo a process called ukutwasa, the gruelling training that an African shaman must undergo in order to become a traditional African doctor or ritual specialist. Most often, the calling to become a traditional doctor is not an easy path.

'When I arrived on the first day the old grandmothers laughed – they said I would never make it. But I knew I would. There were times I thought I was going to die. I was living in a hut in the middle of nowhere and I realised fast that I am not as tough as the local people. I was a weak American. My immune system was not used to the bugs and parasites.'

His lowest time was when he ate goat and developed severe food poisoning.

'I didn't know at the time what was going on. I was just so incredibly sick – I didn't know if I was going to live or die. I took a taxi to a clinic and they told me I would live and the doctor gave me good advice: "Don't eat a sick goat."'

I looked at him again. He was reed thin under the draping of animal skin and beads, and he had sores all over his mouth, body and feet.

He knew by then that an initiation is a baptism of fire, not to be taken lightly.

Stories like this are common around the fire in Botswana. This is the world the Campbell brothers work in. It is far from the realm of 'rational' understanding. But that's why people all over the world are coming here to learn.

People want change. Niall has his finger on that pulse and is living it.

'We are really lucky that we live still side by side with cultures who have maintained their relationship with the earth for millennia. It is these cultures now that will lead the way back to harmony and balance,' he says.

'Most of us live in isolated worlds and are driven by individualistic thinking. We are driven to amass and accumulate. We think of wealth in terms of finances or property – and it is artificial and unsustainable. We are all trying to accumulate and keep. There is no longer flow. This is going to change. We believe that the millennia of experience that indigenous people have should be recognised as a model for environmental and social sustainability.

'Nature is the original law. Change comes when you show people the power of a more connected way of life. When people come on our workshops they may find their views change. We let them sleep a night in the bush; let them reconnect them with nature and community. We show them that they had ancestors who did the same. That is how change comes.'

The weekend was over too soon. I left Llewelyn there for a few more weeks and was due to fly back home.

I sat down on the British Airways flight back to Cape Town. As we lifted off and left the stark plains of the semi-desert of Botswana behind, I found myself seated next to a man I knew well. He was flying home from a work conference.

'How's Llewelyn?' He had a concerned look in his eyes. 'I heard he's on borrowed time and I am so sorry for you all. How are the kids?'

It was as if a dose of cold water had been thrown in my face. It

Wild rapture

was so unexpected and foreign. We had left that world so far behind. Other than the six-monthly MRI scans, it was not a reality in our lives.

'Oh no,' I said, 'you have it all wrong! He is amazing.'

'Oh, that is such fantastic news. My brother-in-law had an astrocytoma and he made only six months. I can't believe he is doing so well.'

He asked where I had been.

I worried that I had a crazy look in my eyes when I told him about the medicine journey Llew was taking and the ceremony we had just done, up in the bush.

'Isn't all that woo-woo weird stuff a bit scary?' he asked.

I thought of the bugs and flies. I thought of last night, singing in a tiny hut that felt as if it was soaring in a charmed sky.

I thought of Henry, heading back on another plane to the cold concrete jungle in South Kensington.

I thought of our next trip to the MRI machine in eight weeks, looming when Llewelyn was finally back home.

I was pretty sure I could feel a bug in my shirt.

'Yip,' I grinned. 'It was totally wild.'

King of the Congo again

'You are still clear.'

Another clear MRI.

The relief flooded through both of us. We walked hand in hand out into the sun. Every MRI was torture. The night before, he never slept. Each scan takes over an hour and then we have to wait for the results. Nerves make me chatter and so I fill the space with random conversation.

This was the eighth MRI so far.

We will celebrate tonight.

'Still no driving,' the oncologist stressed before we left. 'Or swimming alone.'

Llew had made an easy plan between friends and family to get around. Friends were no problem for him, and he had a vast network of friends and colleagues who loved him. Added to that, his parents now lived just around the corner, so his lifting options were extensive.

'This weekend we need to do a feast for the ancestors. Let's do it on Saturday night. We need to give thanks.'

'Only family this time,' I said. Our family was huge. Between us, it could fill a hall.

I was bone tired, working two jobs and parenting, and still making time to write for international magazines – often on health and science.

'I may have another job,' he told me in the car on the way home. 'The agency got hold of me about shooting some more beer commercials in DRC.'

'You think you are up for that?" I asked. 'Kinshasa is hard work, in case you had forgotten.'

King of the Congo again

'I'm not sure, to be honest.'

'It is so stressful there. No roads, all those challenges, and last time there were endless power cuts and you nearly blew a fuse. Is the stress good for you?'

'I am going to think about it,' he said. 'But this feels good. It's been three years. It feels like I can start my life again properly and this is a great test.'

He had been working casually for a while. His reputation in the industry as a director had pulled jobs to him.

He had directed and shot a film of the work he and Niall were doing in Venda with the protection of Sacred Sites. Water sources, mountains and breeding grounds for certain populations of wildlife have for centuries been considered sacred. All countries had sacred sites like these, which were rooted in nature. But as people got more educated, the sense of what was sacred moved away from nature and into man-made churches, shrines and places. As churches, government buildings, monuments to politicians and statues were created, the respect for pre-existing sacred sites was forgotten. The documentary shone a light on these sites and the thinking behind them, and particularly the fight over the Thathe Vondo forest. In this area lies the Mahovhovho waterfall and the Sacred Forest, where chiefs of the Thathe clan are buried. The Sacred Forest is rumoured to be so full of spirits that few Venda people dare to walk through it.

He had also been shooting a few commercials and a series of documentaries, called *Leap of Faith*, with Lisa Chiat and her production crew. It was a series that highlighted exceptional people in this country who were making a difference and taking a leap of faith to follow their calling.

But more than his reputation, Llewelyn was just simply magnetic to be around.

Not just brave, and bold. But deeply intelligent, madly quirky, full of heart and art and honesty and insight. People were drawn to him,

LOVE AND ABOVE

pulled to his shine. There were a few who found him too strong a taste to handle, but most became part of his tribe.

It had been close to three years and his hair had grown back to cover the staple scar. The dent in the right side of his head was still there, making him even more intense and interesting. It was compelling and intriguing. A photographic portrait taken of him in the middle of his radiation treatment was released in a coffee table book called *Jong Afrikaner* (Young Afrikaner) by Roelof van Wyk and Stephanus Muller. Out of the pages stares his face, swollen with steroids, a scar down his head and his lips burned from radiation. The book was a series of portraits of what were described as 'urbanised, creative, engaged Afrikaners who present a challenge to preconceived ideas about Afrikaner values and identity'. He was photographed barefaced, vulnerable and proud – an Afrikaner who was becoming a white sangoma.

While he gathered around him a circle who loved him and his life was rich and full, we were fraying around the edges as a family. The stress of the endless scans was like a long, slow grind that was wearing us down. Money was tight and my part-time jobs weren't really cutting it. I was putting pressure on him to work, and he was wanting to only focus on his path.

Our relationship was becoming increasingly distant, and I spent many nights sleeping in the guest room. He spent more and more time in Botswana and Venda. We were passing like ships in the night.

Air initiation ceremony

It had been over a month since I'd left Botswana after another long week there. I came home floating on air, and left Llewelyn there with his face caked with white kaolin, deep inside another initiation ritual. It was over his 40th birthday, but he had not been allowed to speak much to me. His sister Kath had joined us, driving from Johannesburg, and the three of us had sat on the mud floor and eaten cake. I gave him cards and letters from the children and read him a poem I had written for him.

We stayed for the week, supporting him in his ceremony, and then I flew back.

The mud had long been washed off my toes and the smoke from my hair. The rapture and the magic had been washed out with it.

The cold reality of my life was back.

I was struggling to make ends meet and keep the family afloat and I was single parenting the two of them. Night after night. Homework. Supper. Bath. Story. Bed. I would fall asleep shortly after them, depleted from the day.

Slowly they pulled away from him too, more and more used to his absence.

'I am frazzled,' I told Liz.

'What can you do?' she asked. 'This path is life or death for him. We just all have to make it work and pray for a miracle.'

'I am done,' I told the Triumvirate. 'I can't go on like this, holding down the fort.'

'Yes you can,' they told me.

'I am moving out with the kids and leaving him,' I confessed to

LOVE AND ABOVE

his mother Ingrid over a few too many glasses of wine. 'I have found a cottage down the road, and I think he needs to consider if he wants this path or his family.'

She shook her head. 'No. That is simply not the right thing to do. That is not what we do in relationships, or in families. We fight on. We stick it out. We forgive and we work on it. I know this is hard, but leaving is not an option.'

I knew she was right.

That night I drew a long, hot bath. The kids were tucked up in bed and I poured myself a glass of wine and stepped into the steam and sank down. My phone rang.

It was a Botswanan number. It had been over a month since I had spoken to him.

I stared at the phone for a long time, then answered.

His voice was rough and low.

'It's me.'

'Hi you.'

'How're the kids?'

'We're all good here,' I lied, hardly able to keep the resentment out of my voice.

Long pause.

Then an excited childlike giggle in his voice.

'I have such good news. I can't wait to tell you. Today was literally the best day of my life,' he said.

'Mmmmmm.' I took a sip of my wine, propped my phone up and slipped lower in the hot water. 'Tell me.'

'We got back home out of the bush today. And it was the first time I could eat with a fork.'

I lay back in the hot bath and looked around me. Bottles of shampoo and domesticity surrounded me. Wet towels on the floor, kids' clothes littering the washing basket.

'What?' I asked. 'I don't understand.'

Air initiation ceremony

'I have graduated . . . and my reward was a plate and cutlery!'

'Is that why it was the best day?'

I felt it rise in me. Rage. Dark and angry.

There was a cautious pause.

'How am I supposed to respond to that?' I asked.

Cool it, cool it. Don't lose your cool, I told myself.

Fat chance. 'How about a HOW ARE YOU, SARAH? How about thank you for doing this all alone and looking after the kids? What the actual fuck do you think I am going to say to that? A FORK! FORK YOU.'

The line hung with a long silence.

'Sarah, what is going on with you?'

He sounded disassociated and distant, and not entirely interested in my mental health.

I heard Niall in the background murmuring to him. I raised my voice to make sure he would hear me too.

'Do you even care what is going on with me? Do either of you?'

'Yes.'

'Well, if you would care to know I am not okay. You have fucked off for months now and I am alone. I am working. I am cooking. I am looking after the kids, day in and day out, alone. I am stressing about money and how to pay the bills. I am fixing the fence, cleaning the pool and doing the plumbing. Basically I am fucking mad and I am not okay. And I don't know if I ever want you to come home.'

With each sentence, my volume was rising.

Silence. No feedback. No traction.

'And so I am glad you got a fork today. Good for you! If I was there, I would stab that fork into your hand.'

Silence.

'Are you there?'

'I am. But I am not going to get into this right now. I think it's better if we don't talk for a while.'

LOVE AND ABOVE

Click.

A month of no contact, and then this.

I went under the water and into the murky bath I screamed and screamed out bubbles of rage.

Later that night I finished that bottle of wine and then another and then I passed out on the couch wrapped in my gown, my hair still wet.

I scraped myself up at 6 am when the alarm went off and, after the morning school lift, and with a splitting red-wine headache, I called an emergency session with the Triumvirate.

'When's he back home?' Georgia asked. We were tackling a climb on a brisk walk. Lulu gave me a pack of Myprodol and a bottle of water.

The three of us kept each other sane and safe.

I had told them the fork story during the climb to a few snorts and giggles.

'Supposed to be in ten days. But I am not sure I know what to do any more. He has changed. I can barely recognise him.'

We stopped to look at the view as we reached the top of Camps Bay.

'You mean physically?'

'Yes, of course. Just look at him.'

I showed them a photo taken up in Botswana. Llewelyn was kneeling on the sand floor, his face smeared in white kaolin and his white robes draped over him. His eyes were downcast.

'Holy shit.'

'Yes, okay, ignore the white stuff, but he looks so different. He *is* so different. His hair is long and curly, his entire body is different. But more than that, his personality is different.'

'Could the hair be a result of the chemo tablets he's still on?' Lulu asked.

I nodded. 'Sure, but it's all still weird. His personality has changed

Air initiation ceremony

– I am not sure if it was the surgery, the shock or the work he is doing in his koma path, but he is a different person. I can't relate to him at all.'

We all sat on a tree stump in the sun.

Lulu looked at me, her eyes kind and caring. 'Sarah, do you think he is going to make it?'

The quizzical look on her face stopped me in my tracks. I looked at both their faces. I frowned and took a step back.

'You mean live? Yes, of course he is. You don't?'

They both shook their heads, concern on their faces.

Lulu took my hand. 'No, my friend. No. He is not. We all know that, and I want to check that you do too.'

I heard her words and stared at her. What on earth did she mean, they all knew this?

Then I shook my head. 'You can't know that, Lu.'

'But we do,' she said emphatically. 'We do all know this, and I am worried you are unable to face it. We all know how this is going to end.'

'We don't,' I said.

My girls looked at me with love in their eyes. They both nodded. 'We do.'

Fuck.

No.

What were they saying?

I was so shocked. I stepped backwards. No.

Nobody had spoken to me so directly about this.

'Sarah, listen to me. He had a tumour that will come back. The fact that he has lived this long is an incredible feat. But you need to speak to Murray. We need you to know where this is going.'

Murray was her brother-in-law, so she had the inside scoop.

I shook my head. 'I don't believe it.'

'We know, my darling,' Georgia said. 'That's why we are having this chat with you. We need you to know that Llew hasn't got that long left. The fact that he has made it so far is the miracle. But we will all get through this together.'

The walk back was fierce and small talk filled the empty spaces between us.

'You know I don't accept it,' I told them as we got out of the forest and headed back to our cars. 'And I don't think it's true at all. I have been reading up about it and there are spontaneous remissions. Miracles. This is not a cut-and-dried science. The stuff Llew is doing, I think it's working.'

They nodded. But then shook their heads sadly.

'We know you don't want to hear this. But you must. It is going to happen, and we want you to be ready.'

I climbed into my Subaru and drove off. Not angry. Shocked.

I was grateful that I had such loving friends who cared enough to tell me the truth.

I sat with what they had said. I sat with it for days.

Then I discounted it.

The next week I decided I needed to scrape myself off the floor of misery. My first step was to get a real job. I was tired of living on freelance gigs.

'Go back to magazines,' Georgia urged. 'You're such a great editor and you are ready for a full-time job. Besides which, I think it will give you the stability you lack. Things are so crazy at home with all that is going on. A solid job will give you some support.'

I needed that. I needed an office and a solid sense of self again

'You are right. Look at me. I have let my entire life slide. It's been on hold for the past two years. I haven't written. I have done great freelance gigs for *Marie Claire*, *Women's Health* and the *Guardian*, which were really fun, but I need to get something on the go again.'

The next day I got online and sent my CV out for a load of new jobs. After two years of no replies, I was suddenly in demand.

Liz popped over and spent the night, helping me with the kids and a meal.

Air initiation ceremony

'I am so glad you are getting this happening, Sarah. You need to get something going – you can't rely on Llew to earn any more.'

I nodded.

'But more than that, I feel you need the stability and the normality of a job. It has been a long and crazy journey and I am worried about you. You have two kids to raise and you need to get some systems in place for them.'

'I need to, Liz. I know Llew is pulling away. I am pulling away from him. It just feels as if we are drifting apart and I can't connect to him any more.'

She took my hand.

'Sarah, he is preparing to die.'

I recoiled. Not her too!

'That's not true. We have spoken about this, and he is not. He is preparing two paths – to live and to die. But we are clear that he will live.'

She nodded. 'Well, you need to prepare some things too, okay? Start by preparing yourself to work.'

A week later I was appointed the group editor of a publishing company in Cape Town. I had a corner office in town and an assistant, and I was ready to step back into the world of work.

Holy smoke and spirits

'Sarah.'

Another 5 am call from Botswana. Niall's voice was strained.

'We are flying home today. Can you fetch Llewelyn from the airport at twelve?'

No contact for another week, and now this.

It was a weekend, luckily, and I was starting work the next week.

'I'll be there,' I said. 'Must I drop you at home too?'

'No, I am sorted, thanks. I have lift.'

I got out of the car to meet him and stopped. He looked different. He had lost a lot of weight and his hair was longer. He had a patchy beard.

We loaded his suitcase into the car and he got in and quietly sat down. I turned to Niall.

'Tell me?'

He shook his head.

'Just get him home. We will talk later. He's has had a pretty intense time and he needs to get home and ground now. I am going to leave him with you, just get him back and let him settle.'

I nodded.

All the anger and resentment I had felt just evaporated in the morning sun as I sat next to him. He was a shadow of himself, thinner, his face drawn. He was pale and quiet and he could barely talk. He sat staring out the window, with one hand on my leg. His eyes were vacant.

At times tears ran down his face.

'I am not okay,' he whispered to me, and squeezed my hand.

I put my hand on the back of his neck and stroked it.

Holy smoke and spirits

I stared at him for a long time, and I knew what was going on.

I knew that vacant face. I'd had a face like that when I had the sweat lodge out-of-body experience.

A line from the Leonard Cohen song 'Hallelujah' belted through my head.

I know this room and I've walked this floor.

'Right!' I said. 'You are freaking out. First thing, I am stopping at the pharmacy and getting you some tranquillisers to calm you down a bit and we are getting you home. You need a hot bath and sleep.'

He nodded, head bowed.

I had learnt a bit about medication over the years and I knew that tranquillisers had a way of lowering the frequency of this kind of experience. I had used them as a way of control at times. They acted like a dampener, dulling the intensity of the vibration that touches all your cells when you feel like this. Alcohol works to dull you the same way, but it is not as effective or fast.

The twenty minutes from the airport felt like an eternity and finally I pulled up at the pharmacy. I had called ahead to our doctor and got a script. They were waiting and I paid and left.

He took one in the car.

We got him home. He could barely walk, and I supported him up the stairs. He went into the bedroom and got into bed, fully clothed, and lay there in a half-dream state under the blankets like a small caterpillar in a cocoon.

I lugged his suitcase out of the car, took off his shoes and then went to fetch the kids from their granny where I had left them for babysitting.

They were so excited to see him after so long that they barrelled up the stairs, screaming.

'Dad! Dad!' they called, jumping on top of him.

Then they stopped dead. He was lying still in his clothes, curled into a ball.

LOVE AND ABOVE

He put out his arms to call them closer but they both raced out of the room sobbing.

'What's wrong with him, Mom?' they asked.

'He's so tired. It's been a long trip,' I lied.

'You sure he's not sick again?' Ruby asked.

I shook my head and distracted them with a project.

The next day he was no better. He got up and showered but was walking around the house like a ghost. An echo of the ghost I had been.

I called his mom.

'So, the good news is that Llewelyn is just back home. The bad news is that something is wrong, and he is a bit trippy and out of it all. The thing is I just can't look after him Ingrid. I've just started this new job and I have the kids to look after and we have sports and a project to do. The truth is I can't actually cope with him. Can I drop him at you?'

'Bring him over,' she said.

I packed a bag, helped him down the stairs and dropped him off. Ingrid's warm cheek kissed mine.

'Leave it to me,' she said, squeezing my arm.

'The kids can't see him like this,' I told her in the driveway as they got him inside. 'It's scary for them.'

She nodded. 'I'll make him his favourite dinner and he will be fine.'

The next morning, she called. 'It was a stomach bug, and he is feeling so much better now. He really wants to be at home. Come and fetch him. I think he must be at home with you and the kids.'

I raced over to collect him. He looked the same to me. I knew it wasn't a stomach bug.

'Let's go for a walk on the beach,' I suggested. 'Before we go home. Get your feet in the sand and ground yourself a bit. You look a bit out of it.'

His eyes were wide, and when we got out at the beach he was like

Holy smoke and spirits

an excited child.

'Look at it. It's all so different,' he said with wonder. 'They have changed everything. It is so developed.'

I glanced along the Hout Bay beach. Same buildings. Same carpark. Same beach.

I got him home and called Niall.

'Not the call you wanted. I am sorry, but you need to collect Llewelyn. He can't stay here like this and his mom doesn't know what is going on with him. I do. And I don't want it in my house right now. I am done with all this crazy shit now. Done, Niall.'

The simmering resentment from the months before was rising, along with my voice.

His suitcase was still unpacked on the floor. I emptied it in a pile of filthy cloths and repacked some clothes for the colder climate down south.

'Don't wash those hiyas,' Llewelyn called to me in a strained voice. 'You can't wash the blood out of them.'

I nodded. I knew most of the rituals now and the do's and don'ts of the rites and processes.

I walked across our garden to the ndumba and opened the door.

I dipped my knee and clicked my fingers twice at the threshold as an acknowledgement to the ancestors. Then I leaned in and put his stuff down.

I didn't walk in as I had my period and that would mean a whole other ritual. Blood was not allowed in the ndumba and if you were menstruating you had to run your hands in ash before entering. I was all out of ash, and patience, so I gently placed all of this clothes and bags down.

I looked around the dark room. It smelled of herbs and prayers and hope. Red cloths lined the walls, jars of herbs and medicines were packed high, and a cow hide covered the floor. The shrine sat, lit by a lamp that was always on. It was warm and red, like a dark, pulsing

LOVE AND ABOVE

womb in our garden.

I closed the door and locked it.

When Niall rang the bell 40 minutes later, I walked him down the stairs, bundled in a warm coat, loaded his bags into the car and kissed him goodbye.

Niall looked wary. It had been a long trip for both of them, I could see this, and the weight of caring for him was taking its toll on all of us.

I touched Niall's face and gave him a grateful hug.

'Thank you,' I said.

The next day I dropped the kids at school and drove into the city to work. It was such a relief to be in an office, have conversations about ad sales and deadlines, and join the functional and normal end of society. I tried not to think about the red prayer hut in our garden, and all the hopes it held, and all the prayers it had heard.

After work I fetched the kids from aftercare and the evening ritual began – homework, wine, supper, bath, bedtime story, collapse into bed.

That night, Llewelyn called me. I was standing over the oven with a glove and a pan of chicken schnitzels, checking their colour. His voice was rough and low.

'I am so much better, stronger.'

Hmmmmm.

I checked on the peas, half-listening.

'Your voice sounds raw.'

'I want to talk to Jude.'

'Jude, put that iPad down and come chat to Dad,' I called.

I had the phone on speaker. None of us had ever put a phone to our ears again since the day of the tumour.

'My boy, I need to make you a very serious promise.' His voice came over the air, choked with emotion. 'One day you will have a son and I will be there. I will be there and you will come and put him in

Holy smoke and spirits

my arms.'

I snatched the phone away.

Jude looked confused.

'Mom, can we eat?' he asked.

I nodded, walking away from earshot.

'What. The. Hell. Is. Going. On?' I hissed. 'Inappropriate! Jude is six. He's hardly thinking of starting a family. My God, what are you thinking?'

But a deeper part of me had reacted to a different reason. It was not true. I knew it. *He would never hold his grandchild in his arms.*

'We have been busy since I got here. We spent most of the day doing a pahla.'

His voice was dreamy.

'This has been the most incredible 24 hours of my life,' he said. 'Sarah! My grandfather Oupa Fritz was with me. He entered my body. It was not me you were with or who came off the plane. It was him. That is why I was so confused on the beach. I remembered it from his eyes, 50 years ago.'

'Great news,' I said. 'Better than the fork.'

I wasn't really being sarcastic. I wasn't being dismissive. I accepted it. I had seen things wild and weird enough over the past few years to know that that was what had happened.

He pressed on, his voice choked with emotion.

'You may not understand, but this is everything I have worked for, that we have worked for. I now understand everything. Everything is going to be okay.'

What was the appropriate response?

Should I congratulate him?

I should.

I really should.

I should be the bigger person and do that.

Instead, I felt a rising rage. Black rage.

LOVE AND ABOVE

How dare he?

How dare he tell me that this had been the best moment of his life? Wasn't the fork that moment?

How dare he make Jude that promise, that he would live?

The words of the Triumv echoed in my head.

How dare he feel joy.

I am no longer in this experience.

I am no longer in this crazy shit.

Smash the house. I wanted to.

'Right, kids,' I sang, 'dinner and then let's all cuddle up and watch a movie.'

I turned off my phone.

The big news dinner

Llewelyn's diary: Travels in hyperreality
After three years of clean scans my August MRI last year picked up the beginnings of a regrowth. I was put back on the chemotherapy regime. By April this year and after seven months on chemo the growth had shrunk significantly.

Emboldened by the response of the regrowth to the chemo and Chinese medicine combo as well as yearning to find another way to shrink the tumour I chose to take a break from the chemo for some weeks to see if only the Chinese medicine could make some headway. I will tell them all tonight. Sarah is going to be upset as the results have been good. But I feel I can manage this now on my own.

We have all been invited to a celebratory dinner at Llewelyn's mother's house. Ingrid is a consummate cook and her creative and artistic house is the warm and welcoming home we all gather at. She can turn a chicken into a warm and welcoming dish with the sprinkle of a few herbs and her secrets. His father John was pouring the champagne and warming up the room with his smiles and hugs.

A frosty situation had started to develop between Niall and me. We were the two gatekeepers and there was a distance between us now as Llewelyn pulled further and further away from me, and closer to his teacher and their work together.

I was willing to let him go there. Frankly, it was easier on my heart.

I felt myself pulling away more and more since the tumour had started to regrow. It wasn't conscious. Terrified of what would happen next, not wanting to feel that terrible fear and loss again.

I was totally present, but I felt myself pull away emotionally into my own world. In that world the most important thing was the kids, and making sure they were protected and okay.

I had put away the hiyas in the bottom of my drawer and put my own small shrine at the back of my cupboard.

But I would show up to this, yet another, celebration.

We'd had many of these over the past three years, both in Cape Town and in Botswana.

But the scans were no longer clean.

Murray was there, his tall frame leaning into the meal as he laughed and chatted.

Niall was there.

Llewelyn sat between them, looking serious. He was far from me and had been staying at his mom's house for a few days. I hadn't spoken to him alone for a while.

Champagne was poured and we toasted life. I wasn't feeling it. No joy. No celebration. No lightness.

His father said grace and we all started to eat.

Llewelyn cleared his throat and tapped his glass.

'This is a special dinner,' he said. 'We are all here for a reason and I have stuff to tell you. But first I wanted to ask all of you how this journey has been with me these last few years. I want to thank every one of you for being here, for walking by my side and holding my hand on this. This has been the most exciting journey of my life. And the hardest. But every time I felt my light slipping, one of you were there to hold my hand, lift me up and march me on.'

We are all invited to share how we felt, and we moved around the table, each person sharing from the heart.

I reached for the wine a few times too many to toast each person's words. My head was woozy and a flush had spread on my face by the time it was my turn.

'I am going to say firstly that you have not been easy. You have not been a walk in the park. You have challenged conventional thinking,

The big news dinner

made me run circles, made me drive in circles and write endless articles about quack cures – many of which we have done together. So, I want to thank you for expanding my research skills. But I want to thank you for the adventure. You have taken us all on an epic adventure with you. This may not be the adventure you chose, but you are living it to the full. I see your clear and brilliant spirit. You are brave, you are loved, and we are with you – standing right here next to you.'

When the circle was finished, Niall spoke.

'All of you were with us a few years ago when we sat around the fire and announced to the ancestors that Llewelyn had a path. At that time we were not clear what it was, but over time we tested it.

'He is on the path to become what's called a koma doctor – a doctor of rites. In this work, you must follow the path. The path does take him away from home a lot of the time and that is causing conflict.

'He keeps getting filming jobs and they are bringing money in, but they are not aligned with his path. At the same time, the tumour is back.

'This discussion and dinner was called to let everyone know the seriousness of his path, and to remind you that your job is to support him. When somebody has a path they are in a canyon and there is no other way out. He can't go off and make money some other way. But what I need you all to know is this.

'This is all on track.

'This is all as it should be.'

I leaned back, relieved. Phew. It feels like someone knows what is going on. Someone has a plan.

Llewelyn spoke next.

'I want to make an announcement and tell you all that I am stopping my chemotherapy. We have decided we are going to use only the Chinese herbs and I am going to fully embrace a different way and completely commit to the path.'

His mom said a quiet prayer.

LOVE AND ABOVE

I sat, quiet. My first reaction was disbelief.

Murray spoke next.

'I am behind Llewelyn on this as his doctor. This is a brave decision and one he has not taken lightly. I will be monitoring him and supporting him, whichever way this turns out. His oncologist will be informed. He is not going to be particularly happy, but that is not his choice, it is Llewelyn's.'

Lots of questions followed.

I sat back and felt my heart expand. Pride surged through me. What a brave, special way. To chase the deeper cure, to reach like that for something bigger.

I was scared, and a bit tipsy.

Later that night I walked outside with Murray.

'This could be a disaster,' I said. 'It feels as if the chemo is working and why mess with a good thing?'

He shook his head.

'Sarah, the tumour is now chemo-resistant. It was always only going to work for so long, and he knows that. These drugs will keep it at bay for a bit longer, but eventually it will regrow.'

I frowned. 'But he can have it operated on again surely?'

Murray shook his head. 'No. That won't be possible.'

I stood still for a while. 'What are you saying, really?'

'Sarah, this is his way of choosing how he wants to die.'

Bile rose in my throat. My heart pounded. That was the word nobody had said for years. It hit me like a sledgehammer in stomach.

'Llew has bought himself three years with you and the kids through all the work he has done with Niall, but the regrowth – well, there is no stopping it now. He is choosing his own path now, whether he knows it or not. I know it. Niall knows it. We are walking the path with him. We all are. You have to be brave now.'

'What can I do?' I asked.

'You have been doing it all along. Life happens in the small

The big news dinner

moments. Keep him busy. Engage him in the detail of life. Make him cook meals, let him work, make sure his is spending time with the kids – make sure he is living fully for now.'

I hugged him tight. I didn't want to let him go and drive home with Llewelyn at my side with a growth in his head.

I didn't want to load the kids in the car and then unload them on the other side.

I didn't want to have to sleep on the couch again.

I didn't want to watch this happen.

We were living on borrowed time.

I was scared.

That night I lay on the bed in the spare room and closed my eyes.

What if Murray was wrong?

What if he could find a way through and heal this?

Is this the worst mistake ever? Is the magical just a fantasy?

I can't tell any more. Both felt so real to me then.

I felt disorientated, as if the rug and certainty of life had been pulled out from under me again. But I knew I could not run away. No more than I could have in that room with the chickens.

There is no running away or stopping this.

I felt this panicky, rising fear that neither the wine nor the celebration of the evening could dismiss.

I sat in the feeling, wondering *what* it was I was so scared of.

Life.

Death.

Everything that was coming.

I fell asleep with my pen in my hand and the words in my diary.

I am strong.

I am a warrior.

Part 2

The coma

The endgame

'I have a sinus infection,' he told me as he shuffled through the house.

His voice was thick and slow and strange.

I glanced up at him sharply. He was in his brown dressing gown, looking worn and messy and tired. Him, not the gown. When I had bought the gown for him to ride out the cold winter it was plush and looked like a glossy mink.

His face was lopsided, and one side was not moving. His eye was drooping, and his mouth pulled to one side.

It was the tumour.

I knew it instantly.

'Sit down and I will bring you a hot lemon and honey,' I said in the Calm Voice. He pulled his dressing gown tighter against the winter chill and sat down with a heavy thud on the couch.

Nobody would hear my voice shaking or my heart pounding. I had got control down to a fine art over the past few years. What I felt inside by no means showed on the outside. Inside my heart was pounding. I had to move.

I stood up fast and walked into the kitchen and turned on the kettle, aware that my hands were trembling, my body was showing it, as I slowed my breathing.

Dread.

I moved like a robot, cleaning the Oscar juicing machine. He was on an alkaline diet, one of the many alternative modalities we had tried over the years, which involved juicing entire lemons. Someone knew someone who had stayed clean for years on that regime.

Green juicing, Chinese herbs. Acupuncture. Reiki. Reflexology.

LOVE AND ABOVE

Ozone therapy. Vitamin C therapy. Mistletoe. He had drunk peroxide, fasted, done the Art of Living, the Flower of Life, TM, and meditated more and more. He had prayed, danced, cried, cleansed and ketoed. He had journaled and done Family Constellation work and iridology. He had cleared his chakras, past lives and karma. He had done Vipassana, TRE, BodyTalk and Kirlian aura images. He was a koma doctor.

Short of visiting John of God in Brazil and having psychic surgery, there was possibly not one alternative thing he had not explored.

But fate seemed to be bigger and more powerful than all of that. And we were down to this. I gripped the counter.

'I am going to pahla in my ndumba. Can you bring it there?' he asked as he shuffled through the kitchen, limping now.

'Mom, what's wrong with Dad?'

It was just weeks before Ruby turned nine and she was watching him like a small mouse watching a cat, her natural intuition for fear and her knowing on full alert as he shuffled through the house. She turned to me, her eyes wide.

'Just a cold,' I told her. 'I am making a hot drink. Want one?'

She glared at me. 'Don't lie,' she said. 'Is it back?'

'I am not sure,' I said. 'And I promise you I will tell you the truth as soon as I know. But it looks like it may be.'

Her small face crumpled with pain.

We both watched as he walked across the garden, opened the ndumba door and slowly disappeared into the dark room.

No, no, my mind was screaming.

He is going to be so disappointed. She is going to be so disappointed. This can't be happening so fast.

I was scared to look at him, scared to see in his eyes the dull light that showed me his brain was swollen.

It wasn't a sinus infection. It wasn't a cold. It was the one thing we had avoided. Run from and kept away.

It was the endgame. I didn't yet know I was only going to have a

The endgame

few more weeks with him, with us both alive.

Later that week I sat the kids down after dinner and delivered the news as best I could. Jude was seven and had moved into Grade 2. Llewelyn was staying at Niall's.

'Guys, there is bad news. The tumour in Dad's head growing again and you may have noticed he is a bit odd.'

'He looks weird, Mom,' Jude said.

'Will he have another operation?' asked Ruby.

'He probably will. We are going to get the best treatment for this and he may go back on chemo, or even go back for surgery.'

'Could he die?' Ruby asked, her voice clear, demanding and angry.

I nodded. 'He could.'

She sobbed herself to sleep in my bed, the three of us cuddled up together.

Llewelyn's diary: Travels in hyperreality

A scan ten days ago revealed that in this period the tumour had grown again and quite fast. This has come as a big shock and yet it was always a possibility.

The tumour was causing some discomfort and headaches, which I assumed was a bad sinus cold. I am also back on steroids to ease the swelling and side effects of having a bit of 'mass' in my head.

I am back on the chemo.

I surrender.

I will do three more rounds of chemo and then scan in September.

The hardest part of now is to surrender to something I cannot control even though I've been so 'at it' and doing so much work on myself for these last few years.

I feel humbled and devastated in equal measure.

The magazine boss

My work had become the place I most wanted to be and now I was racing between work and hospitals.

I was the group editor of a publishing company run by a family. If you had to take all the craziest and wildly A-type people and put them into one family, that would be this one. The family opened a publishing business that rang on a promise of advertising.

The mix was sheer chaotic madness. I loved them all, but it was cowboy publishing, crazy, unpredictable stuff. It gave me a lifeline. It was to be my home for the year of descent into madness.

In my working life I have chosen jobs for many reasons. My first job I chose because I had a dream of becoming a journalist. I was fresh from university with a degree in African politics and a major in waitressing late nights at the Hard Rock Café and spending days on the beach.

I headed off to London to break into the glamorous world of magazine journalism. First on my list was *Elle*, where I got as far as being a receptionist for two days. Finally, I hooked a job as a rookie journalist at one of the biggest financial publishing companies in the world. *Euromoney* was on Fleet Street and the CEO had an Irish name that was impossible to wrap my tongue around, Padraic Fallon, and he was to interview me personally.

He took an instant liking to me. Not for any particular skillset I possessed in writing, but simply because I was South African. My 'interview' consisted of him lighting up a cigar, offering me one, putting his feet on his messy desk and asking me all about Cape Town, beaches and wine. I was primed with my CV, all my writing samples and a newly bought power suit. He didn't even ask for my credentials.

The magazine boss

'Do you know anything about the financial markets?' he asked. I shook my head. My father had been in construction and money was never talked about in our house.

'Fantastic,' he said. 'You can start tomorrow. That way you will be able to simplify the ideas for the readers.'

I certainly did. Starting on the obituary column and then moving to the bond reports for the Asian markets.

Now I was back at another magazine. The pace was ruthless, the job demanding and the company – well, complete mayhem.

A magazine deadline is a sacred thing. It is the moment when a year of work all comes together. It was a print deadline, and the magazine was running late. There was a massive event in Johannesburg that weekend and I had to sign off the proofs, print the magazine and get the stock couriered to the event in time for Saturday night.

It was a race against time. Nothing unusual for a magazine business.

I was just walking a very fine line between doing my job and caring for Llewelyn and the children. His condition was deteriorating, and walking was difficult for him now.

I was racing off during my lunch hour to join him at doctors' meetings or another scan.

On many nights, now, he would stay at his mom's house down the road. I asked him to because I wasn't sleeping. I was scared. I was scared every night that he would die and I would wake up and find him cold and stiff next to me.

So I would wake up and check on him all night.

What would I do? How would I find him? Who would I call?

'Call me,' Liz said. 'I will call the right people.'

I was so scared of his dead body.

I was scared of death.

I was scared of life.

I slept less and less. I wasn't really noticing. I was living on nerves, caffeine and stress. I would race home after work every night, feed the kids and do homework. Then I would get them to bed and cram in some extra work.

Often, I would go and see Llewelyn and bring him home for a night or two.

It was a tense, nervous grind.

One night, I drove slowly along the street towards the house after a late-night event at the office. I knew the babysitter was there and the kids were in bed and asleep. I would have to take her home.

I looked at the other driveways in my street with longing, wishing one was mine. I wanted to go anywhere but into my front door, where so much pain and defeat waited.

The next week, when we celebrated Ruby's ninth birthday, his face was thick from steroids and his eyes uneven. He was barely able to get up and down the stairs to our house; one leg was dragging.

His sangoma work seemed to have faded away and he spent little time in his ndumba. He became more and more distant and detached.

That Thursday was crunch time. I raced to the printers to sign off the proofs. I parked at the industrial park on the outskirts of Cape Town. It was fenced in, alongside the highway.

'We need about an hour to get the final prints,' the floor manager told me. 'Come back at 3 pm.'

I had two hours to kill. Truthfully, I wasn't feeling that well. I had a thumping headache I could not shake, and I didn't want to have to drive back out there later.

I called the office and told them I would wait. I knew myself. Often, the best way for me to kick a headache was to run it off. I took my running shoes out of the back of the car and kitted up for a jog around the office park. Running is my relaxation and meditation. The first twenty minutes are usually tough as I find my stride, but then my breath comes to me and the pace eases up and it feels like magic.

But that day, it never happened. Twenty minutes passed and it just got tougher. I was tired, and my legs felt like lead. I was running through

The magazine boss

mud. But I pushed and pushed to 40 minutes.

By the end my throat was raw and my hands shaking. But I felt alive.

I signed off the magazine and drove back to the office.

That night I felt terrible. My throat felt like razor blades were slicing into it.

I pulled into my driveway in a cold sweat.

It felt like flu was coming on. I fed the children, stuck them in front of the TV and got into bed. At some point they must have taken themselves off to bed.

I woke early and dialled my mother-in-law.

'Ingrid, I need your help. Again. I am actually so sick,' I rasped. 'Please can you fetch the kids and take them to school for me tomorrow? I will fetch them later.'

'Stay in bed,' she told me.

My office was not impressed. I called them from bed and asked them to get my work laptop delivered to my house. Luckily, I had signed off the magazine and it was on its way to Johannesburg. There was not a lot I had to do but I didn't dare be 'off work' for a day. The driver arrived with my laptop and I worked a bit.

I slept most of the day, with a fever, but somehow managed to get up and collect the children and get them home in the afternoon.

That night, Llewelyn came back. The bug had moved down my throat and into my chest. It was tight, and hard to breathe.

I called my gal Lulu. She'd had flu and had been moaning about her throat.

'Lu, this bug is the pits. I've got the same thing as you,' I rasped.

'Razorblades in throat? Check. Sore chest? Check.'

Lulu always knew how to make me feel better. We chuckled about our days and I fell into a fitful sleep.

That morning I packed the kids off to school. The house was quiet and empty. I crept up into the study to check on Llewelyn.

LOVE AND ABOVE

I inched the door open just a crack and paused, half expecting to hear nothing. But I heard his rhythmic breathing.

He was alive.

I climbed back into bed, back into my feverish sleep.

At about 8 am I woke in a massive coughing fit. Something shot out of my chest and got stuck in my breathing pipes. It was a thick, sticky ball of phlegm – and it was totally stuck in my throat. I could not breathe at all.

I stood up and staggered towards the study. This was crazy, I was choking on a ball of phlegm. A final desperate push and it dislodged. I collapsed to my knees in shock. Thick, choked guttural sobs.

That was close.

Too close.

Strangely close.

I called my mom.

'Mommy, I am really sick and I am not coping. I need you to fetch me and I want to come to your house.'

She came over, loaded me into the car.

I had left Llewelyn, sleeping still. I left the beds unmade and the house dirty. I took only a few clothes. I took the work laptop and my phone.

'Get into bed,' my mom said. 'Nothing a good sleep and a nice steam won't fix.'

Later, I made some calls and made sure the kids were looked after. I lined up all the lists. Sent an email to my office. Cancelled a dinner that night.

Bad timing. Wrong timing. The wheels were coming off with Llewelyn and I needed to look after him. I needed to look after the kids.

I could not get sick.

I had left him sleeping and hadn't even said goodbye.

This is the last thing I remember.

An epic freefall

The next few hours I have pieced together. I have no recollection at all of any of this.

The next morning, I was on the phone to my medical aid.

'You need to get me to hospital,' I told my mom. She is from the 'just drink water and it will pass' school of medical support.

'Calm down, Sarah. You are tired and you have flu. You just need to rest. You are being totally irrational,' she told me.

But I had already got a pre-authorisation number.

'I need a letter from the GP to be admitted. Let's go.'

I walked out and stood at the car.

She took me to our local doctor, who listened to my chest and said it wasn't good, and it sounded like bronchitis. But I was insistent. I wanted to go to hospital.

Eventually my mom backed down, and the doctor booked me a bed.

I don't know what drove me to do all this, but it was some deep inner intuition, and it saved my life.

Finally, my mother agreed, confused and a bit angry. She left me at the hospital reception while she parked, and I checked myself in.

I had a lung X-ray that night and it showed a small patch of pneumonia on my right lung. I sent some text messages to friends and to work telling them I was in hospital and wasn't feeling good.

The next day Mom arrived at the hospital. The older lady in the bed next to me was very concerned, and beckoned my mom over.

'I am worried. Your daughter is very sick,' she told Mom. 'She is talking gibberish. Last night they found her in the shower, fully dressed with even her shoes on. Something is wrong.'

Mom was surprised. 'She looks fine!' she said.

But she spoke to the physician to check. He checked the night chart which confirmed that I did, indeed get dressed and climb into the shower last night. He was concerned but said I seemed okay. But he booked me in for another chest X-ray.

It had a surprising result. Both lungs had a thick, white snow all over them. I had full-blown pneumonia. In fact, I had what was is fondly termed a lung blackout and was in full respiratory failure.

Things moved quickly from there.

I was rushed straight from radiology to high care, where I was hooked up to a load of machines. An hour later I was taken to ICU and hooked up to a ventilator.

I was immediately put into an induced coma.

I didn't see the ICU doors as they opened. Nor as they closed. I didn't know that they were going to close on me and on the life I had known for the past 36 years. I didn't even know that I had entered a room in which I was going to have a fight. This was going to be the fight of my life. For my life.

I knew none of this. I was too far gone already, my brain and organs starved of oxygen.

I didn't exist outside those ICU doors any more. I had left all that behind. Nothing came through. Not my children, not my family, not my husband.

I had left him sleeping that day. I would never speak to him again.

It was to be over a month later when I would finally check my cellphone to see a message from him, sent on that day. It was the last message he ever sent me.

My darling. You need this rest. Relax. I will take care of everything. Just sleep. When you feel better I will book you a massage.

Coma stage 1: The world of nightmares

I am being held in an experimental institute and that they are doing experiments on me.

I am in a dystopian reality. I am in the is the worst, dodgiest place in the world. It is a broken place. There is garbage everywhere and long hospital corridors filled with glass.

There are reams of cables and electrical sockets. Broken fluorescent lights flicker overhead. There are people walking all around. They are all strangers. But who am I?

I am dying ever so slowly. I die by suffocation. I can't breathe. Doctors are all around in this strange place, but they are doing other strange things. They are measuring liquids and testing equipment. They are all ignoring me and my screams.

It's a test. Doctors will not let me die. Will they?

This is getting stranger and stranger.

Now I am lying on the floor and they are all walking by. They want to see how far I can go before they save me. How scared I am. I want to pretend I am not scared but I am fucking terrified. I don't want to die. I want to breathe but I am suffocating. Again.

Another nightmare. A man who comes and goes. He's always in a different outfit. He wears rubber gloves. I am so relieved when I see him. It must be a reality show. I am on a show. He is an actor. Why else would he be there? That's it – I am in a death reality show.

My mind is sharp and analytical. I am smart. I tell myself this. I can win this game.

But how did I get there? And what is the game? In fact, who am I? I have no idea. I am just somebody dying while nobody is watching.

LOVE AND ABOVE

In fact, there is no real thought in my head at all. I am just trapped here. In this twilight world between worlds. I have no idea why I am here. But I don't even question that.

And then the nightmare repeats.

Then I feel myself floating upwards on the ceiling. I can look down but I don't want to see what is on the bed and so I float to other places. I got to other wards and along empty rooms. I don't want to look at any of the people in beds, they have a sad and bad energy, I only want to look at the air and so I move to the windows. They are closed.

I want to get out of here.

But who am I?

Actually, I don't know who I am. It's not exactly scary, but it's uncomfortable. I am just floating around the hospital. Floating means having no roots, no place. I have nowhere to go.

The next thing I notice is that things are not happening on the horizontal plane any more. There is no sense of left or right. There is only up and down, and I keep moving up.

There are buildings. They are modern Gothic. Vertical. Steep. I traverse the world in a vertical way. Up and up. I am moving upwards. There's no ground.

Is this a vertical hotel? It's very stylish and there are people in black tie. There's a cocktail bar, green plants hanging down over the edges. But the place is not important. What is more important is that the world is going on around me but nobody notices me, or that I am dying.

The drugs that were keeping me unconscious were creating on-going nightmares as my brain tried to make sense of what was going on in my body. The drugs usually used are barbiturates, which act by slowing down the brain's metabolism and reducing blood flow to the tissue.

A body in a coma is highly vulnerable. You can't cough, can't breathe, can't move, and the body can't control blood pressure or pulse

Coma stage 1: The world of nightmares

rate very well. Added to that, I was on a ventilator and running fevers because all brain function must be shut down in the deepest levels of sedation.

Of course, I knew none of that. I was just trapped in a world of endless nightmares.

I am in a loop after loop after loop. Dream after dream. In every loop I am suffocating to death. Slowly.

I'm going to keep you updated on Sarah with this Facebook thread as we are overwhelmed trying to take over her life, and handle Llewelyn's last few weeks.

At the moment Sarah is in ICU, fully sedated, and on a respirator. She has been in a coma a week now. They will do lung X-rays again tomorrow and know how she is doing. The doctors are really confused by what is going on and are testing her for a superbug. We are all very confused and are trying to manage the kids as well as Llewelyn.

We are telling Llewelyn what's happening to Sarah without traumatising him. He understands she is very sick. We are all trying to contain it so he is not upset by calls as he's in a very fragile space at the moment and is in the final phase of his cancer battle.

Llewelyn has moved to his mother's house and Kath has moved to Cape Town to help care for him now. Both Niall and his best friend Richard have moved in to assist. He is comfortable and has a team of people looking after him.

My mom, Jayne and I are looking after Sarah and the kids. I have moved into her house and am with them. We all go every day to ICU to see her, but Mom has barely left her side.

Hopefully better news soon.

Stage 2: Out of the body

Day 8
*Just heard from the doctor that they feel she has turned a corner! The X-rays are better, still it's there, but improved! Going now and will send her all your love.
Liz*

Day 9
*Mum just been to see Sarah. She has barely left her side. Doctors say it's going to take a while. She was quite disturbed, think it's so scary having all these pipes down her, but she is unconscious so won't remember it.
Liz*

I have shot out of the hospital.

It was so fast I didn't even notice it. One second I was hovering somewhere in the corridors with fluorescent lights, the next I was shooting through the air. It was as if I was being pulled forward by a cord to my chest, so fast and furiously it was like a rush of wind and light and freedom.

In real time I have no idea how long I was trapped in these endless buildings and hospital corridors. I still had a vague idea of who I was then. I was . . . well, someone. A person who was scared.

I was still somewhere near my body, the one lying that bed.

But I have left that behind me now. It is such a relief. I have left the hospital and that body on the bed behind me now and I am somewhere else entirely. There is no noise of machines or doctors here. There are no buildings.

I am soaring far away from all that in the sunlight and the world

Stage 2: Out of the body

is more familiar. There is a horizon. There is land and sun. I am in the clouds and looking down like a bird in flight.

Now I am no one.

I have no name.

I am not a body and not a mind. I am just a thought. I am nothing. I am just like a feather in the wind.

I am floating across landscapes and terrains.

Freedom and light. Bliss.

I am not in a city familiar to me any more. I move over some familiar lands, over the sea, but I have moved on now, far away.

I am feeling and sensation. I have a mind that is observing. I want to look around. So I fly through the clouds. I swoop over the fields.

I do not know I am in a coma.

I am just a lone soul with no name, simply floating. I am content to be here. I can control where I move. I can swoop lower, play with the birds, move through clouds.

So I have thought and I have feeling. But I have no past. The world of nightmares is gone, and it is out of my mind. Perhaps that was yesterday, perhaps a thousand years ago.

I have no real agenda. The only thing I have is a vague feeling of discomfort. Like I don't really want to be here, and I have somewhere to go, someone to find.

But I am not sure where I want to be.

Day 11

Not great news, there has not been any improvement. Her doctors are worried as they don't know what is causing this infection in her lungs. They are doing a scope procedure tonight to try and find what's happening in her lungs and why she's not improving. The head surgeon had a meeting with us and said it is a medical anomaly. The hospital held a special emergency panel looking at her case, is this some extreme superbug, are other patients at risk. How did it happen?

She is resting, which is what she needs.

LOVE AND ABOVE

I am spectacularly aimless. Like a cloud on a summer's breeze.

But not quite.

Something is pressing me forward. Some elemental desire. It was so slight it was barely an impulse. Just a passing thought.

I must move on.

I am drawn to a particular farm. It slightly resembles a Tuscan summer. Warm fields full of trees bursting with fruit. Green fields and a house on the hill. There is a man there and I am drawn to him. He is a father. There are children with him.

I float down to be with them. They are building this beautiful wooden house. It is a home for a family. A father and two children. I want to be with this family. I spend a long time there. I am in the sun wrapped in my fantasies of another life.

But they do not see me. They do not love me. I will come back another time and visit.

I must move on. I cannot stay here. Not forever. They are not my people.

Stage 3: Limbo

Day 13

Jayne and I just left Sarah. She is stable, though very agitated. The nurse told us things can improve and then go down a bit with this, we need to just take it a day at a time. We are going to try and get Llewelyn to her bedside.

I am still in the world of earth, and I find another family.

I travel upstairs. I can move easily and with just a thought. It is that simple. I glide through the house. It is such fun. I can glide. It's not like flying, it is more just moving. Flying has a sense of freedom and of air. This is just like sliding from one place to another.

I can feel my mom here somehow. She is close by. I feel desperate tears. I can feel her slipping away from me. I pull away.

I will never see her again.

Upstairs I find some children. I play for a long time with them. They are busy with computer games and watching television but they don't notice me.

There are people in this house but they do not acknowledge me or talk to me. I am not sure if they even see me. They move around me. Talk to each other, but not to me. Nobody can see me or hear me. I am nameless and faceless like a ghost just watching. I am powerless.

I know that I do not belong here.

This is not my place.

I feel one emotion strongly now. Frustration. I want to fly away and be free.

What started as a blaze is threatening to incinerate me. The feeling is all consuming.

LOVE AND ABOVE

I am blazing light.

My will is that I want to get out of here.

Day 15

Another rough day today, didn't progress as much as we wished for — we are hoping Llew's visit will help her spirits lift to turn a corner. They have also done a scope into her lungs to extract more phlegm as they are still unclear what the actual virus/issue is that is causing her to be so sick.

Jayne

Stage 4: The ceremony to say goodbye

Llewelyn came to the hospital and sat with Sarah tonight. He can't walk any more as the tumour is growing fast and so he is in a wheelchair, but he sat with her and stroked her hair. I think she was waiting for him to come, and she seemed to relax and rest with his presence. This may be what her immune system needed to start to fight back now!
Liz

I am out.

There is no transition. I do not travel. I am just somewhere else. Out of the house. I feel blissful freedom. I am in a new realm. This is not the real world any more. I have left farmlands and horizons far behind. There are no houses here.

This is only a space for spirits and other beings.

This feels good. It is light and good.

Day 17

We are doing all we can on the outside of this coma, but Sarah is deteriorating. I am reading all your messages; we did Lulu's meditation technique. We talked to her of Jude's hugs, played her videos of Ruby's concert recital. Jayne has strapped healing crystals under her bed in ICU. We play her the Kundalini music sent by Trish and the prayers from New Zealand. Her oxygen levels are down lower tonight.

We are keeping the kids loved and supported. They are at school and the school is amazing and know what is going on. They see Llewelyn almost daily after school and lie cuddling with him. He sleeps most of the day now, and eats. We have openly discussed what is happening with him and that he is dying. We

LOVE AND ABOVE

have only told them their mom is a bit sick and needs to rest. They seem accepting of that.
Liz

I am in the spirit world now. It is vast and endless. It has a physical space. The best way I can describe it is like an endless landscape of trees and warmth. There is grass like rolling green hills and trees speckled in the landscape. It is warm and I feel a rush of relief.

It feels ancient. It feels warm and welcoming and I can hear music pulsing, like song.

They know me here. Even though there is nobody I recognise I know that this is a place where I am welcome. I am loved. I feel my name whispered, even though it is not the name I use. The relief is so great I want to weep with joy.

I have no real idea about what happens after you die. I believe deeply in a God and in a power far beyond me. I have read a thousand books on heaven, on spirit paths and on soul journeys. I call on angels all the time.

But none of this is what happened to me. There was no light. No tunnel. No friends and family to usher me into the Great Welcoming Hall. There was no hall. No angels. No God.

But there was this. And this was one of the most real and visceral things I have experienced. This beautiful, gentle place filled with love. There was music just filling my ears with a peace so empty and vast.

This was a place outside of the physical world. It was a world of souls.

My soulmate is here in this realm.

I can feel him. Llewelyn.

My husband. He is here and I know him. I think I found it because he was here already and he called me here.

I can't see him but I know he is here. He is with 'the men'. And they are far from me. They will not let me see him.

Stage 4: The ceremony to say goodbye

This spirit world is a private world. Everyone who is here, is here for the two of us. This is their role. They are all strangers to me. But they are here for this reason alone.

We are here to say goodbye.

A tribe of women come and surround me, singing a slow and beautiful song. They are African and their skin shining and black against the white cloth they wear. There are red beads on them and some of them wear white headdresses with red beads on their heads.

They take me by the hand and lead me to a tree. They are preparing me for a ritual. They dress me in pure white. The song is so beautiful it wells in my chest and pours out of me.

My parents are long forgotten. I have no name.

I know they want me to say goodbye to my Llewelyn. He is going away. The men have taken him, and I know they are preparing him.

'It is a great battle,' the women whisper to me. 'He has to fight the elephant, and the elephant will take him. But he has to fight it still.'

They are preparing him to die.

This is freedom and bliss. I am loved. It is gentle. I am being held and soothed.

'Let him go,' they tell me. 'This is his honour.'

I want to. This feels so right. I want to sink back into the warmth of their arms and let the tears glide hot over my face. I want to give up. I want to give him up.

He has a journey to make. I know he is ready. He stands as the men sing to him. He accepts the robes and the spear. He is proud to be given this honour.

I know he is there. I can feel his ease with this. But he cannot feel me. His vision is on the path ahead and he cannot see me.

But it is me who cannot accept this.

No, I scream. No.

I will not let you go. No. No. No. No.

The women hold me back as my rage and my pain pours out. I

cannot let him go. I am a warrior. I can beat them. I can save him. I am stronger than them. I will not abandon him.

I am fighting the women now. I stand up and take a spear.

No, I say. I will not let him go alone. I can save him.

'Llewelyn!' I scream. 'Wait for me.'

'Where are you?'

I scream over the hill.

Day 18

She is not having a good day, as her oxygen levels are down and temperature up. We've managed to get permission for Llewelyn to see her again tonight, hoping this will help, but his condition is getting worse by the day and this may be the last visit.

On the outside it is totally crazy! Friends are flying down from all over to say goodbye to Llewelyn. Ingrid is cooking and welcoming them, but she is exhausted.

My mother is furious because Llewelyn showed the kids a photo of Sarah hooked up to all the machines. There is the Cold War of the mothers.

We have had to get lawyers in to discuss what would happen if they both don't make it. This is seemingly impossible and something we don't want to face. We need your prayers.

Day 19

She had a tracheotomy done, which is a more long-term solution to her being on a respirator. They have identified an organism they found in her, a bacterium that may have caused a massive secondary infection. She is now on other course of antibiotics. The kids are struggling and missing her.

I know he is close. Can he feel me? Don't go with them. But the singing of the men is loud. It is rising to a chant. It is building in fervour. It is a war cry. I can feel my power. I am strong. I am powerful. I have to find him. I have to find him. I have to get out of here.

When I look back over my coma and the places I visited I sometimes wish I had taken the peace that was offered to me. I see

Stage 4: The ceremony to say goodbye

now with more lucid clarity that what was being offered was not my death, but his.

The fight was over already. But I did not know that.

I wanted to fight. I wanted to fight everything and everyone.

Day 21
Sarah took a bad turn last night – she pulled her tracheotomy out in the middle of the night and had to be resuscitated by an emergency doctor. It took over 20 mins to bring her back and then she had to be fully re-sedated again and they had to insert a new one. Not good news.
Jayne

Day 22
Sarah is struggling so much today, she has been fully sedated again, which is a setback. Even in the coma all those tubes and pipes are freaking her out. She has no idea what's happened, but still she is fighting the tubes, so very traumatic for her and those watching.
Liz

Llewelyn sleeps most of the time now. Sometimes he wakes to eat or get taken to the bathroom. Pain meds are zonking him out too. Mom in bed with flu/exhaustion. Please no visitors, we are all exhausted. Kids are solid and their friends are a huge support.
Kath

Stage 5: Floating away

Day 23
Another setback today, they've had to redo her tracheotomy a second time this morning. This time she pulled it out with her teeth it seems. This is so tricky as they want to slowly bring her back to consciousness as we know it is the last few days for Llewelyn, but they are not able to stabilise her. They are trying a new approach now, so hopefully this will work.
Liz

Floating.

Aeons ago I left the world of men, of form and substance. I am floating away in the universe. I know it is the universe as I can see stars and lights. I move through them. I know the lights are other souls, like me. Formless and free, just bright, blazing, clear lights.

In the empty, vast place I have been in for so long, this beautiful music filled it, like a hum and a song.

Before I had been a star. A being made only of light and energy. Formless and free. It was so peaceful and easy. There were no strings or attachments. It was just endless eternity. It was bliss.

And then, I felt as if something touched me out there, beyond the stars. Something changed.

Interestingly, in the 'real world' something was happening that very night.

Day 24
Friends we are holding a collective breathing session and meditation for Sarah tomorrow night. Please all join. We are really fighting for her now and trying to help

Stage 5: Floating away

her find her way back to us.
Liz

We are joining you tonight, praying for Sarah and lifting her up before God – here from the far corner of the world in New Zealand.
Guy Bullen

That night they had scheduled a meditation and prayer for me. There was one in my own home in Cape Town and friends from all over were invited. But all over the world people who knew me joined in. My sister Trish in Johannesburg held one at her house, where everyone gathered. My brother in New Zealand joined in with his entire church. Friends in the USA, Costa Rica and the UK joined. Not just family, but friends, churches, groups and people all around the world joined that night.

At the same time, they all sat for a while and lit candles and prayed. My sisters Liz and Jayne led a meditation at my house sending me love and healing.

I have always believed in prayer. It does not matter to me where it comes from – God, the universe, the earth, a higher power – any prayer is pure love. And I felt it.

Because deep and far away, I heard something in the darkness. I heard voices calling me.

It wasn't as literal as that. It was an awareness that came to me.

Though the dark space I had a clear, distinct, and real thought. It cut through like a beacon calling me.

I know that this was the turning point for me. I have read many NDE stories after waking up and I know that this was the moment I made a choice.

I had a conscious thought for the first time.

It felt as if there were two threads pulling at me.

One thread was my spirit, and that wanted to float away and be free. The other was my soul and it wanted to be somewhere. It was

LOVE AND ABOVE

being called back, down and back to family and love.

It was the soul calling I finally heard.

Come home, it said.

So, one clear thought entered my being. It was the thought that drove me for the next week until I finally woke up back in my body.

Back.

Get back.

Get home.

And that thought changed everything.

I needed to get back. Away from here.

The limbo. The purgatory. The surrender. The passivity. The waiting. The dying.

I was getting out.

And NOW.

Day 24

Thank you to all who shared tonight's beautiful meditation with us. The love and amazing energy from across the globe was felt. So many joined us from far and wide. This is the most powerful medicine ever.

Stage 6: The house at the end of the world

Like a beam of light, I was shooting back to earth. Just that single thought made it happen. It was fast and effortless; I shot through the universe at the speed of light.

All of a sudden, I was on another plane. This plane was more familiar to me. It was on earth and there were forms and figures.

This time I ended up in a southern state in the USA. I could see the land and recognise it. I could hear the accents. I felt relief to see forms I knew – rivers, boats, trees and voices and people, rather than just a vast emptiness.

Day 25
Sarah is much calmer today. We need her awake now, it has been so long. If she stays like this they will discuss removing the trachea, which will be amazing so she can breathe alone. It will bring her back on to our side of the 'wall'.

I was fighting my way back to my world. It felt like a huge physical and mythic battle. I imagined ancient warriors who left home to travel the world. They had to fight epic battles, wrestle gigantic beasts and cross impossible rivers.

I still have no name or any sense of who I am. But now something has changed. I know one thing.

I know I love someone and he is fighting for his life and I need to see him. Who is that again?

Llewelyn.

Yes.

I know his name now, but not mine.

LOVE AND ABOVE

Day 26

Been a very hard day for Sarah, she is fighting. She has been so long in the coma that its very fragile to bring them back. The doctor says the recovery rate is only 10%. We need her to live.

They are trying a new approach to bring her out. It's a very sensitive time now, so we are all just holding our breath and hoping she can find her way back now.
Liz

I am back in the world of nightmares. I tear myself closer by sheer force of will. Nightmare by nightmare.

I am in a house at the end of the world. The house is dirty. The bed is unmade. Dirty dishes are in the sink. Llewelyn is there. He is in the house, but I can't find him.

'Where are you?' I scream out. 'Helloooooo!'

I am strapped to a metal bed in the middle of a cold room.

I want to get back to my husband now. I want to get the fuck out of here. He is here, but he keeps moving away. He is out of my reach.

I am strapped to another motherfucking bed. I am getting tired of this now.

But my brain is more active now. My brain is working, figuring this out.

Then suddenly Llewelyn is with me.

'Shhhhh,' he says and puts his hand on my forehead.

I sob with relief.

'Don't fight. It's just the end of the world. We are both here now. And it is all going to be okay.'

'Stay with me,' I say.

But he shakes his head.

'I have to go, my queen. I just came to say goodbye.'

He leans down and kisses me on my lips gently.

And then he is gone. I can't see where, because I can't turn. I am tied to a cold steel bed. Even my head is strapped down.

Stage 6: The house at the end of the world

He has left me alone. I have battled the world for him, and he kissed me goodbye and left me.

Stage 7: The spirit guide comes

I have watched movies about people waking from a coma. They opened their eyes and the fog cleared.

It's nothing like that.

Waking up from a coma is not a singular event. It is a process of waking up for a few minutes, fighting your way out and into consciousness, and then slipping back under.

In the real world I was still in a deep coma, but the sedation was being slowly lifted.

What I didn't know was what had been going on in the real world. The world where my body lay, breathing through tubes and machines.

I didn't know my mother had sat an almost constant vigil at my bed for three weeks. They had talked to me. Sang to me. Played me music. Brought video recordings of my children. Slapped me. Tickled my toes. They had washed me. Brushed my hair. Tried to talk some sense into me. They had put up a photo wall of people who love me.

They had screamed at me. Read me books. They had talked and cried.

I had been too far away to hear any of it.

I had been in a coma for three weeks.

What had happened to my body was severe. I had lost close to twenty kilograms. I was hooked up to a life support machine and one of the side effects of complete inactivity is oedema. This is roughly a swelling of all your extremities. I had compression machines moving the fluids out of my legs, but they were still swollen like fat sausages and I was hooked up to feeding tubes and machines.

I became aware I was in a hospital. I knew there were machines

Stage 7: The spirit guide comes

and doctors. I knew I was somehow sick.

I knew nothing else. Although I was somehow back near my body, I still had no idea I was in a coma.

I was just a body in a hospital bed fighting for my life and moving in and out of my body.

But now more awareness came, and there was a man with me.

He was short – far smaller than me – and if I had to guess I would say he was about five foot tall. His hair was a long bob. The fashion magazines would call it dirty blonde with natural highlights. It hung down on either side of his face, tangled and knotted and unwashed. He was about 45, but he was gnarled and earthy. He looked as if he had come out of a forest a long time ago. He was neither male nor female, but I somehow knew he was a male.

He was standing by my bed, and he took my hand. I knew this man was not a doctor. He felt of life, and of the earth.

He looked at me directly. Deep into my eyes. This was strange because it felt as if it was the first time this had happened in a long time (and I was actually in a coma still).

'Greetings, and welcome back,' he said.

Formal. Old-fashioned.

His voice was gravelly and rough.

'I am a healer, and your sister Jayne has sent me to you.'

Jayne. I knew that name. That was the first name I had heard I could relate to. I didn't have to ask who she was. I knew I had a sister called Jayne. I knew her. It made sense that she had sent him to me. I trusted her.

My brain was fried. I was moving in and out of my body, floating down hospital wards at times and moving back into the bed at others. I was deranged and dangerous. But I knew the truth on an instinctual level.

I was a bit suspicious. He was not a calm, benevolent presence. He moved in a fast, jerky way. He didn't have wings. His skin was a deep brown from sun and life. But what he had told me rang true.

'Please help me get me out of here.'

At that stage I did not know I had a tube down my throat and could not have actually spoken. We didn't need to speak. I knew what he was saying. He knew what I was thinking.

He smiled.

'You will. In time,' he said. 'All in good time. But not yet.'

So the Forest Man stayed with me.

If I track time back, I know how long he was at my bed. It was about four days. He didn't do a huge amount. He sat with me during my darkest hours. He put his unearthly hand on mine.

'Just wait,' he said. 'You will get out of here. When the time is right. It's not quite time yet.'

'I am ready,' I sobbed.

He would nod.

'When you are ready, it will be done.'

I was nasty.

'Fuck off,' I told him. 'I don't need you. Leave me.'

He smiled.

'You are so full of spirit,' he said. 'Don't waste it now. You have a long road ahead of you. You have lots of things still to do.'

I tried to trick him.

'I need to hold your hand, please,' I said. 'Just untie me so I can hold your hand.'

I planned to pull my tubes out. He smiled.

'Let me die,' I told him once.

But as I said that, I knew I was lying. There was no way I was going to die.

Not one chance. Not now.

I had no idea why I needed to live. I was still not aware of my family in a constant vigil at my bed. Nor that I had two children, left at home. I was just a sick person in a bed who wanted desperately to live.

Stage 7: The spirit guide comes

I was still not awake in the real world. I was in a coma and fighting to come out. I would slip between the world of nightmares and this calm space, where I was back in my body, and he was with me.

Stage 8: Waking up

Then he left me. I was still fighting to wake up and moving in and out of consciousness.

But before he did, he bent down, he kissed my forehead.

He stroked my hair.

'What do I need to do?' I asked.

He smiled and looked me in the eyes. 'Have more fun.'

I lay for a long time, looking at him.

Have more fun?

Those three words caught in my throat. I wanted to spit them out. They were so strange to me. Rude, even.

Fun?

What was that? This was not fun. Life was not fun.

How dare he?

How simply dare he tell me that?

That was the last time I saw him in that in-between world. He has come back to me later, in years since. But then, he simply disappeared.

The ICU at night is a terrifying nightmare world. Not even Dean Koontz or Steven King could imagine the nights of terror.

It was cold and late at night. I was chained to a bed and I was freezing cold. If felt like an icy underground parking lot. It was industrial with strips of fluorescent lighting. Broken lights were all around and cold metal beds. I was in some of them with a flimsy blanket over me. The cold was bone-deep and biting into me.

Stage 8: Waking up

It was a hospital. But it was more like a night shelter where the homeless slept. It seemed there was a price to be paid for being there that night. There were so many prices. My first price was that I was chained to the bed. From the icy cold an even colder metal chain was wrapped around me wrists, tying me to the bed. I was not sure how I got here. Did they not know who I was?

But actually, I didn't even know who I was.

Who was I?

Even writing this, years later, I feel that feeling and I want to just shut down this page. Turn it off. Turn away from the cold and the lights and the chains. Turn away from being a nobody tied to a bed.

I was just a night-dweller lying in a cold bed, alone. I could not talk. I wasn't sure why yet. But I was silent. There was something blocking my throat.

Then a nurse came up to me through the gloom. She started washing me down with a sponge. It was cold water. Who was she? Who was this freaky bitch from the Twilight Zone washing my pits?

'Okay, young lady. None of your mischief tonight,' she said

The slow cogs in my slower brain were turning.

She knows me? Tonight?

Have I been here before?

What was going on? Where was I?

Another nurse came and the two of them held me down. Then a male orderly. They talk about me.

'She's at it again.'

'You wash her.'

They turned me onto my side.

I was naked. Wet with cold water and getting colder by the passing second.

I wanted to talk. Why couldn't I?

LOVE AND ABOVE

I slip seamlessly between nightmare and reality.

I am in a broken-down hospital wing.

No, I am in a police station being locked in a cell.

No, I am at crazy carnival party with drugs and sex.

No, I am chained to a bed and I am going to die.

No, I am at the party but the police are chasing me. We run and run.

I slip into a sordid club. People are having sex all over.

I had no conscious idea of who I was. No name. No place. I was just a person trapped in a bed against my will.

It is as if I am driven by a deeply primitive impulse. Fight.

Gone was the Forest Man. Gone. Gone.

Angels come in many shapes and sizes. That night, another one came. A nurse. She sat at my bed and stroked my hair. Then she started to sing softly. Church songs. I knew them. They were in English, then Afrikaans. All the while she stroked my hair and soothed me, like you would a wounded animal or small child.

I turned into her hand, desperate for the touch. Desperate for kindness. Desperate for anyone who could help me.

'Please,' I whimpered. 'Help me get home.'

There are more angels all around me. They are foggy, but I know them. Not close like before. Just there in the room, watching me. They will not let me die, but I must trust.

Daylight. I open my eyes

My sister Jayne is sitting by the bed talking to me. She has a huge smile on her beautiful face, her blue eyes shining.

'Sarah,' she says. 'You are a very, very lucky girl. '

In all the weeks it is the first thing I hear.

Stage 8: Waking up

Lucky? Why?

I was back in advanced mathematics and a problem had been put on the board. A complex word sum. I just had to figure it out. Lucky.

I fall back under.

Part 3

Carve the doors with bones and flesh

Dream fever

She is walking towards me across the ward in the morning sun. I know this person. This is my mom. I am okay. Someone knows me. Someone loves me.

She smiles as if this is the most normal thing in the world.

'Good morning, darling. Look at you awake!'

'Mommy,' I rasp. 'What happened? What happened to me? Why am I here?'

My mom is not talking. I don't think she could have. She walks behind me, probably to cry, and strokes my head. The sheer effort of sitting has wiped me out. I am wet with sweat. I am freezing cold. I am naked. I don't even want to look down. I know I am not going to like what I see. I know there are a million tubes attached to me. I can feel a nappy on. I can feel a catheter pull as I move my legs.

'Mommy, what happened? Why am I here?'

'I just told you, darling,' she says.

I frown. She did? When?

'Just keep repeating it.' The nurse is talking over my head. 'It will take time for her to understand.'

Mom sits by my bed. She looks tired. So tired she is pale. She has more lines than I remember. She is stroking my head.

'The kids are fine' darling. They are home. Just focus on getting better.'

'I don't understand. Why am I here? Did I have a car accident? Are the kids okay? What are their names again . . . ?' (I am sure I have kids.)

LOVE AND ABOVE

'Please take me home,' I whisper.

'Shhhhh, darling,' she says. 'Don't talk.'

I grab her hand.

'Don't you dare leave me here. They are pigs. All of them. I want to go home now.'

A cold wind is blowing though the place. It must be an underground shelter of some kind. I can hear someone moaning and screaming in the bed next to me. I can see an old man with tubes coming out of his nose. He looks dead. He is naked with only a thin sheet covering him. I realise that I am naked too. I am naked and chained to a fucking bed. I have no idea who I am or why I am there.

Murray is next to me. I know him. He is my doctor. He is also my friend.

'Why am I here?' I ask.

'You need to rest,' he says.

Liz is by my bed. She is crying. She is laughing.

'Oh Sarah,' she says. 'We knew you would make it!'

I am confused. Make what?

What happened to me? Have I been sick? But feel stupid asking again. I know I have asked before, but I just can't understand it. Why am I in a hospital? With a tube in my chest?

'We are all just so happy to see you awake.'

She has a box of food that she shows me.

'It is all your favourite things. A cappuccino – decaf. A sandwich. Chocolate.'

I have feeding tube down my nose. I look at the food and can't understand what it is. I shake my head.

I lean closer.

'They raped me last night,' I tell her.

Dream fever

She freezes.

'Who?' She looks confused. Her movements are slow. Like she is approaching a wild horse.

'The pigs,' I say.

'Pigs? What, in here?'

'The police. They raped me right here.'

She nods. Puts down the box of food.

'You are safe here, Sarah. Look around. This is an ICU ward. There are no pigs. Or police. Just doctors and nurses.'

My brain is processing this information. I see the branding – Netcare. I know the brand. She must be right.

A bit later I see her standing at the nurse's station. She is talking to them and they are all looking at me. This confuses me. Why do they know my sister? Is she in cohorts with them? They are all plotting against me.

How long have I been here?

Sunlight. It is day and I slowly wake up. Or did I ever sleep?

My mom didn't come. The nurse was a liar. She lied. I am alone.

Liar liar liar liar liar bitch I will kill you with my fucking teeth. You were not an angel you are the devil. Liar liar liar liar.

Did I have a car accident? What happened? Why am I here?

A nurse comes over.

'Good morning,' she says. Then she starts to take measurements. She pricks my finger and tests my blood.

My nose is dry and I can feel a tube up my nose. My chest is rising and falling.

Cuffs. I am cuffed to the bed. I look at her.

She shakes her head.

'Don't try any of your funny business with me,' she warns. Then she goes back to the business of measuring.

LOVE AND ABOVE

What the FUCK is going on? Why am I in a hospital? What has happened?
I start to fight and thrash in the bed. They hold me down.

I see one with a vial and syringe. She jabs my arm. A slow calm spreads over me and I settle back down. A tranquilliser. I know that feeling. Oblivion. I like it.

The most amazing news – Sarah is wide awake, they are about to take everything out – the breathing apparatus. Our meditation and love worked. I saw her earlier, she is very emotional and fragile, coming to terms with what's happened.
Liz

We are waiting for my doctor. They told me he is going to take out my tracheotomy and feeding tube. I am not sure what that means but I can feel a pipe in my throat. It doesn't really bother me but they have told me that I have been trying to pull it out. That is why I am tied down. I can't remember which one he is. It feels like we have been waiting for hours and hours.

Finally, he walks over. He chats to my mom. It is like they are old friends. She looks at him with grateful eyes. She knows him. They hold hands for a second.

Then she walks over and tells me she is going to get some tea while they do the procedure. I don't want her to leave. I can feel the panic start.

'You will be fine,' she says, and looks away. But I know she is lying. She is scared.

They sit me up on the bed and it is very quick. A few nurses are around me helping. I can't sit up even. My muscles are not strong enough. They must hold me.

I want to ask a million questions. Like how will I breathe now that the machine is going to be taken out? What if I can't breathe?

But I can't talk and so I just let them get on with it.

I don't feel a thing and before I know it they are turning me

Dream fever

around and lying me down on my bed. The doctor is patching up my throat with sticky plaster.

'I can't breathe,' I whisper. I can feel the panic. It is sweeping over me like an army of ants. It is going to drown me. The machine breathing for me has gone. I can't breathe.

'You are breathing,' he says.

I am?

'I can't—' I say.

I start choking and gasping. Half of the air is coming through a hole in my throat. I am not sure where the rest is coming from.

'Help me. Help me,' I say.

The nurse gives me a shot in the arm. I feel a warm calm sweep over me.

'Just relax,' he says. 'You are fine. You are breathing just fine all on your own. You don't need the machine. Your body knows how to breathe. It is doing it just fine.'

Does it know?

'Don't try to talk,' he says. 'You have a hole in your throat and won't be able to.'

He puts his hand on my shoulder.

'Sarah, you cannot try to sit up or get out of bed. That is why we have to keep you strapped down. I know you want to, but you can't. You need to understand that during the coma all your muscles atrophied, and they are not going to work for a while. You will need a lot of physio to learn to walk again. So do not try it. You can hurt yourself badly.'

I feel my eyes fill with tears. I look over to the screen by my bed. There are photographs of two children. I am sure they are mine. I know their names. I grab my mom's hand.

'Don't leave me here another night,' I beg.

[line break]

It is 5 am. I can see the clock on the wall. The night shift nurses are

LOVE AND ABOVE

leave and the day shift nurses arrive. I just lie staring at the ceiling.

A younger nurse arrives. She knows me.

'Good morning, Sarah. And how are you doing this morning?'

'I want my mom,' I whisper.

She nods.

Soon.

I shake my head. I start to cry. I snap my teeth at her.

Liar. You are lying. Liars. Liars. I start to fight. Nurses run over to restrain me. But the younger one is calm and kind.

'Sarah, what do you want?' she asks.

Why does she keep saying my name? As if I don't know it?

'I want to go to the bathroom.'

'You do? You think you can walk to the bathroom?'

I nod.

'Okay,' she says. 'Let's see if we can get you sitting up.'

I nod. No problem, sista. I lift my head.

'Just wait a bit.'

She calls three other nurses over.

'Don't do it. She will bite you again,' the one says.

The nice nurse looks at me. 'Will you bite me again?' she asks.

I feel a tinge of pride. 'No,' I whisper. 'I will not.' Again?

'You will not try to rip your needles out this time?'

I shake my head vociferously, trying look contrite. I know that's the right answer. This time?

'If you do, Sarah, you can hurt yourself very badly again. Do you hear me? We don't want that to happen, do we?'

I shake my head. *Oh, just get on with it already.*

She is moving tubes and things. They untie my arms.

They hold my arms and pull me. I have no clothes on. I don't care.

'Now sit up,' she says.

My brain works, but my body is immobile.

Dream fever

They are watching me. This is a test. I must pass it.

I fail. I cannot sit up. I cannot move.

'Okay, let's help you up. One – two – three – lift.'

They hoist me into a sitting position in the bed and swing my legs off the edge. The effort is immense. They are panting.

I am shaking now with the strain of just sitting. I know my body is being held up by the four nurses. It weaves and bucks. Sweat runs down me in rivulets.

'Now stand up slowly, Sarah.'

Oh no. I know already I cannot.

I shake my head. I can't.

'You can,' she says. 'Just for a minute. Let's get you in that chair and we will drain your lungs again.'

Two male nurses take my arms. They brace themselves.

She angles a chair next to the bed.

I nod.

All together they get me into a standing position and swing me around. It is terrifying. I cannot stand and I know it.

They lower me into the chair and I can see them moving around me, moving pipes and tubes and needles. A sheet is put around me.

I am sitting in a chair and I am naked, sweating with fear.

My entire body is convulsing just to try to hold my head up and stay upright. Sweat is running into my eyes and mouth, despite the freezing air.

The kind nurse crouches down in front of me.

'Do you know where you are?' she asks.

I want to have the right answer. I feel I should know. I shake my head.

'You are in hospital, Sarah. In the ICU ward.'

'Do you know what happened?'

I shake my head.

'Do you know what month it is?'

LOVE AND ABOVE

I don't.
'What year?'
Nope.
'How old are you?'
I whisper.
'I want to get back in the bed. Please help me.'

The ICU torture chamber

'Ruby and Jude are coming to see you today.'

My mom is with me, reading a book. She is very excited.

'Mom, the woman next to me died last night. And her baby.'

'Shhh now,' she says. 'You will be out of here soon.'

I look over at the pictures of my children on the wall by my bed. Jude's goofy face is munching a cupcake. Ruby is beaming at me. There are notes written by them and drawings.

How long has it been? I have no idea.

I am not excited. I am detached.

They come through the door cautiously. Small blonde heads hesitant. This is the first time they have been allowed into ICU and it is no place for children. This is a place where people die.

I fake a smile. They move under my tubes and hug me tight. They give me some drawing and kiss me all over. It is taking every single ounce of my strength.

I turn to my mom.

'Take them out of here now,' I rasp.

I finally get my cellphone back but my fingers can't work it.

'I want to see Llewelyn. Why has he not come to see me?'

I try to turn it on. My fingers are not working, and it takes a while. I call up a message.

'Let me help you,' my mom says.

I shake my head. 'I need to do this. I need to know I can.'

Words don't want to form. My fingers don't want to move. I am sweating with the effort.

Llew Where r u.

LOVE AND ABOVE

Come
Come
Plee.
Lov you smuch

The countdown begins

'We need to take you to see Llewelyn.'

Liz is at the door of my hospital room. Behind her are two well-built nurses. I eye them suspiciously.

I have been released from the ICU and moved downstairs into a private room two days after my tracheotomy was removed. I got here yesterday.

Now Liz is here. She has a tog bag in her hand and is pulling out some clothes. Mine. I know that sweater and those Levi's jeans.

'Let's get you up and dressed.'

'I don't know if I can – can't he come here?'

'No, Sarah, he can't.'

'Why?' I ask. 'And why isn't he answering his phone? I haven't spoken to him once. He hasn't called me, Liz.'

I am whispering. Tears are pouring down my cheeks again.

She sits down next to me as the nurses shuffle around, moving drips and lowering the bed.

'Sar, he is not good.'

'Is he going to die?' I ask

She nods.

'When?'

'It's soon now and you need to see him.'

I nod, my hands shaking. My brain is slow, I am trying to understand what this means. A foggy confusion clouds my mind.

'He will be okay,' I console her.

Liz shakes her head gently and holds my hand.

'No, he won't.'

LOVE AND ABOVE

The nurses move around me and they get me dressed. It is torture and the sweat is running off all of us.

At this point I can stand up if someone gets me into the right position, and I can take a few steps, but that is the most I can do. So, they have to roll me around to get some warm winter clothes on.

All the while they are talking to me like I'm a baby.

'Right, now, lady, let's get your left leg into these pants. Nicely done. Now we are going to get it up over your bum. Annnnnd lift.'

It was a massive effort but finally I was the in wheelchair, bundled up warmly and on my way to the parking lot.

I looked back at the room as the door closed. I was out. Freedom.

I was wheeled through reception and into the parking lot. A thin wintery sun lit the sky.

Liz's convertible Audi was there. Not the easiest car to get into, but she had two strapping male nurses to help her hoist me up and into the low-slung seat.

I was going home.

No, wait. I wasn't.

'Why hasn't he called me?' I asked.

'Sarah, he's bad. We moved him out of your house about three weeks ago and into Ingrid's house, in the guest room downstairs. He can't walk any more, and he spends most of the day just sleeping.'

'What about the kids?' I rasped. 'Are they seeing him?'

'I take them to see him every day after school. They have been part of it all along and watched the decline. He isn't awake a lot now. But when he is he's eating like crazy, it's the steroids that are making his so hungry. But how he can't really chew so we have to liquidise all this food. Kath is making him the most amazing smoothies.'

'I will look after him.'

'Sarah, I want to prepare you. He is terrible. Niall and Richard have both moved in and are looking after him around the clock. The house has been so full of his friends that Ingrid has taken herself to

The countdown begins

bed for a few days now.'

'I have decided he must have the surgery,' I told her. Talking was a real effort. I was exhausted from it.

She didn't reply, so I turned and started out of the window. We were winding up the side of the mountain through the sweeping pine forest that stretched from Newlands to Hout Bay. I loved this drive. I opened the window and closed my eyes as the cold air hit my face.

Alive.

But still in between worlds. I felt as if I might just lift off, lift out of this car and soar above the forests again.

The cold air was good. It was keeping me alert and focused.

We turned down into the valley and pulled up outside my mother-in-law's house. Liz stopped the car at the gate and turned to me.

'Sarah, you must listen now. This may be goodbye. Llew has been slipping in and out of consciousness. He has not got long left. Everyone is in total denial, but Murray and I had to meet with everyone and tell them. We need you to see him and just say goodbye in case it happens fast now.'

I turned my head away, blocking her out. I didn't want to hear it.

She pulled her car up close to the front door and got the wheelchair out. I knew this house so well.

John stood at the door with Kath, his face hollow.

There was a stunned silence all around as they watched the struggle to get me out of the car and into the wheelchair. They lifted it up and over the steps, up into the house.

Each one bent down to kiss me.

I was spent already. So very tired. Detached. I wanted to see Llewelyn but nothing was landing on me.

I was tiny and frail. Two words nobody would ever think would be used to describe me.

They wheeled me into his room. I could smell him. The smell of his skin and being hit me from the door. Sweet. Spicy. Familiar.

LOVE AND ABOVE

I sat quietly waiting. He was in the bathroom and there was an epic struggle to get him off the loo. I could hear him shouting and grunting.

'Leave me.'

Kath was manhandling him and finally he was put in a wheelchair and wheeled out.

His face was swollen from the steroids, grotesquely, like a balloon. One side of his face had collapsed. One eye big, the other small. I was scared suddenly.

Liz wheeled him close to me and eventually our two wheelchairs touched. We sat, knee to knee, both in wheelchairs. His eyes were vacant and he looked down at his hands.

Everyone left the room.

Even in my deranged state I saw some dark humour in it.

'Well just look at the pair of us,' I rasped.

But he didn't. His eyes were downcast. He did not look at me at all.

I grabbed his hands desperately.

'Llew, I will not let you go. I will not let you die. I need you to fight this. Get on the phone and get the surgery. Now. Tomorrow. They can take the tumour out.'

He nodded. He held my hands tight. Then he squeezed them both.

I want to tell you, it is hard to be emphatic when you are whispering.

But he wasn't there. He was somewhere else.

But then he bowed his hugely swollen head, and kissed my hands as he held them.

He dropped his head into his hands.

'Sore. My head. Get help.'

I was scared. Confused.

He started groaning in pain.

The countdown begins

Oh God I was stuck. I was wedged in, with his wheelchair in front of mine.

I couldn't call anybody. I couldn't talk at all. I couldn't walk. He couldn't walk.

We sat there in silence. Just his groans.

'Help.' I tried to whisper louder.

Nothing came out of the huge hole in my throat. No air was moving over my windpipe. I was muted.

We were both trapped and alone in a room.

His moaning got louder and he was gasping.

Eventually, the slow cogs of my brain started to move.

I looked at him and started to giggle again.

'You can talk! Can you shout for someone?' I whispered. 'Call them.'

Immediately he let out a roar. 'Mama. Kom gou (come quickly). Niall!'

Seconds later, the door opened.

Llewelyn was slumped over one side of his wheelchair now, crumpled over in pain. More people came into the room as we still sat – knee to knee.

'Get him to the car,' one person said.

'Grab his bags,' said another.

There was a flurry around me as he was wheeled out of the room.

I sat alone in the empty room. Finally, Liz came to find me.

'What's going on?' I asked her.

'They decided this morning to take him to the hospital for his last days to manage the pain.'

'I think he must have the surgery,' I said.

'Let's get you in the car and back to the hospital,' she said as she wheeled me out.

This time, Niall picked me up and carried me to the car and put me in it. I hadn't seen him for months. I had banned him from my house. I had cut him out, angry and resentful of his closeness. Mad about everything.

But when he picked me up, I breathed in his sweet, smoky smell tinged with snuff. I held on tight and put my head on his chest.

'I am sorry,' I whispered.

He put me into the car, leaned down and kissed my cheek.

'Pull through,' he said.

The white Audi pulled out of the gate with Llewelyn in it.

Behind that, my sister's blue Audi followed, with me in it.

I looked behind me as Niall stood in the driveway watching us all leave. It was to be the last time he would see his student and friend alive.

As we pulled out of the gate, I made my move.

I yanked her handbrake up.

The car jolted to a halt.

'What the hell are you doing?' Liz exclaimed. 'My God I nearly went through the windscreen.'

'Turn right, Liz. I am going home.'

She chuckled.

'No you're not.' She grabbed into her purse and waved a document in front of me. 'You see this? This is a slip that allows you to be out for one hour. You are going back to hospital right now.'

She pulled off.

I pulled the handbrake up again. She sighed with annoyance.

I tried to open the door and climb out. It was futile. I couldn't stand, so what exactly I was going to do was unclear. But it felt like a resistance.

She pulled over and yanked out her phone. She had my doctor on speed dial.

I was leaning half out the car now. Weaving and bobbing, unable even to pull myself back in.

'Either you get back in the car or they send the ambulance here

The countdown begins

to fetch you. Which is it?'

She grabbed my arm and yanked me back in.

I slumped back in my seat, with hot, angry tears. I punched my fists against the seat, then the dashboard, then her.

To her credit, she never wavered as she clicked the lock on all the doors.

'I want to go home,' I sobbed.

I was literally 400 metres from my very own house.

My bed. My sunny room. My couch. But it was getting further and further away from me now as we drove back towards the hospital. To that terrible room in that dark ward with fluorescent lights and cold floors. I was retching now, deep guttural gasps coming from me.

Take me home.

Take me home.

I panted. I cursed. I fought.

When she pulled into the parking lot at the hospital, they were waiting for me. The surgeon was standing with the head nurse.

My sister pulled up and they strolled up to her car and opened the door. Two nurses pulled me out of the car, not entirely gently. One of them jabbed me in the arm and they swiftly seated me on the wheelchair that materialised behind me.

I felt a delicious warm oblivion spread though my veins. I leaned back and let them take me back in, but not before I spat a thick ball of spit, right in their faces.

I learn to walk

'Sarah, I am waiting.'

I am on a Zimmer frame like an old, stooped granny, inching down the long hospital corridor with a nurse trailing me.

Step. Step. Step.

The psychiatrist is waiting for me at the door to my room, looking at my chart.

I must walk back.

I am determined to learn to walk again.

She sits on the chair as I go through the laborious process of getting back into bed. I will not accept help. I need to do this myself.

'I need to learn to do this again,' I tell her.

She nods.

She has me on so many drugs right now and I just love her for it. She is my most favourite person and I just want to hold her hand and thank her. Does she have more now?

'Sarah, I have two complaints from the staff about you,' she says. 'Two formal complaints. Again. You were found crawling down the corridor.'

I nod, eyes downcast. Sometimes having no voice is helpful.

'You could have really hurt yourself trying to get out of bed. You are just lucky you didn't. But that is not why I am here. We have a tricky situation to address. We feel you need to go home, and yet you are not medically sound, and we don't want to discharge you. But there are legalities that need to happen.

'Your husband is in a coma at Vincent Pallotti and you are the signatory on his living will. We are prepared to discharge you to attend

I learn to walk

to this, with strict conditions. One is that you will need a live-in nurse to look after you.'

I punch the air with joy. I am getting out!

'Your sister is doing most of the paperwork right now to discharge you, and is getting your medication sorted. She will take you home today.'

I literally sobbed with joy.

Outta here, I text Lulu. My fingers are just starting to work again as my fine motor skills are slowly coming back. I still can't write or hold a pen, but I can slowly construct a text message of a few words.

Yeah! she replies. *Love you.*

We get in the car. I turn with a grin.

'Home,' I rasp.

Liz grimaces. 'Erm, not yet. I can't take you home, we need to go past the other hospital first. The one where Llewelyn now is. You need to sign some paperwork and I think you should see him and maybe say goodbye.'

'Right now?'

'I am so sorry it can't wait. They are keeping him on life support, and he didn't want that, and so you need to sign the documents to remove him from it. And I am sure you want to see him.'

I don't.

I sit silently the whole drive, my eyes and mind vacant.

Kath, Ingrid and John are waiting for me with a nurse, and they help me out of the car and into a wheelchair. I hold Ingrid's hand for a brief second. None of us talk much.

They wheel me into the hospital reception. I catch sight of myself in the reflection of the glass doors for the first time. I have avoided looking at myself in a mirror for all this time. All I have seen is my skeletal legs as I've tried to move them.

The vision is so confronting I look away. That's not me. I am close to six foot tall and stacked with muscles I have earned over years

LOVE AND ABOVE

of sport and training.

But in front of me sits an old and bent woman. Tiny. Frail and in a wheelchair.

My hair is a matted mess, standing up all over but scraped back into a braid.

I stare again, intrigued by that person. I look so very old.

I am wheeled into a lift and down a corridor. Intensive Care Unit.

The door opens and we sanitise our hands and Liz wheels me forwards.

There he is, on a bed in the middle of the room.

Unconscious and hooked up to pipes.

'Just sit with him a while,' Liz says as she parks me at his head. 'We all need to go to the meeting with the oncologist. You don't have to be there, but we will need you to sign the forms.'

'Can he hear me?'

'I think so. He is semiconscious and he does react, but the swelling on his brain has meant it is shutting down. Talk to him.'

Then she turns and leaves me alone with him.

I sit trying to calm my breathing. Breathing alone is a skill I have just relearnt. The voice of the physio is in my head.

'In. Hold. Out. Hold.'

Calm down. Don't panic. You can breathe.

I am choking even before she gets to the door, but she doesn't see. Choking. I have fought so hard to get out of an ICU and I am back in one.

Can't breathe.

Panic.

The noise of the machines is drilling into my head.

Beep. Beep.

The sound of a ventilator pumping up and down.

Help me, I text her.

Get me out of here.

I learn to walk

No reply.

I sit, just fighting the panic. I am so scared to be here. Back here, just another ward. The noises, the nurses, the machines. I sit and sit. Even sitting is a huge strain for me and my muscles are spasming now. I can barely hold myself up and finally I slide down lower to get support for my head.

I feel hot pee run down my leg and pool under my bottom and then drip onto the floor below me.

'Oh God I am so sorry. It just took so long.'

Liz is running up to me. She has just checked her phone. She sees the pee on the floor under my wheelchair. It is long cold and I am sitting in a wet, cold patch.

'Nurse,' she calls. 'Help us here.'

They clean me up as best they can.

'Just get me out of this room,' I hiss.

She pushes me out, into the corridor where Ingrid, John and Kath are waiting.

I need to give permission for his living will to be in place and that means they will take him off all life support and drips.

'Is this the right thing?' I ask Kath.

She nods. 'It is.'

'What about the surgery?' I ask

'It's too late for that.'

She puts her arms tight around me and kisses me on the head.

'You need to go home. We will be here with him.'

One last goodbye

We knew it was happening that night. It was close and I had been kept informed all day.

I was home and back in my own bed with a full-time nurse. There were friends or family looking after me 24/7. I could not stand up alone or sit for long. I could walk, but not move from sitting to standing. I was surrounded and held by Liz, my mom, the kids and the Triumvirate.

I finally got online and slowly typed a letter of thanks on Facebook. My fingers did not want to go to the keys I wanted, and it came out garbled.

thank every one of you for sending the love that somehow pulled me thrrugh. i know that my mom;s relentless love kept me going through the darkness that felt like it had no beginning and no end. I am still processing what on earth hapenned to my life. but my deepest gratutude is simply to be alive.

I had been to see him the day before and sat next to him a while as his chest heaved and rattled. I whispered to him. Stroked his beautiful blonde hair and kissed his warm rosebud lips.

I tasted him and smelled him deeply.

I knew it was goodbye. Even though I had expected this moment for three years, saying goodbye was harder than I ever imagined.

Everyone kept telling me to release him.

'Tell him it's okay to go, Sarah,' they urged.

So, I whispered that in his ear.

'It's okay to go, my Llew,' I said. 'Time to go. Go off on your

One last goodbye

next adventure. I will be okay. The kids will be okay. We love you. Go up to the angels.'

I so wanted to mean it. I so wanted to be that big person, calm and accepting. But I could not. I almost choked on the words.

Instead, my heart just wanted to scream out. I wanted to shake him and cry – DON'T GO. Wake up. Please, please don't go. I just can't bear it. I can't bear the thought of not speaking to you first thing in the morning and last thing at night and twenty times in between every day.

I can't bear the thought of you not being there to calm me, or to hold my hand during a movie. Or rub my feet while we watch TV or sit and play PlayStation with Jude. I can't bear the thought of not hearing your footsteps running up the path before you burst through the door. I can't bear the thought of you not standing next to me at the kids' birthday parties and helping them with their homework in your patient way.

And so I breathed him in one last time. I kissed his lips. I licked the salty sweat on his neck. I rested my finger in the strong dimple on his chin.

And then I walked away.

The next day I screamed. I lay on the floor alone, once the kids were out the house and beat my hands on the floor. I knelt and kicked and screamed. I beat the floor with my fists and shook and sobbed.

No sound came out of my mouth – I was stifled by a hole in my throat, but I was screaming. If I had been at an Irish funeral I would have keened and beat the coffin. I would have wailed like a wild beast. I wanted to smash the house.

That when I saw it. Grief.

Grief is wild. It is uncontained and uncontrolled and uncivilised and I wanted it. I rode it all that day. I think I may have been riding it all along.

But the next night it was time and his family gathered with Llewelyn by his hospital bed.

LOVE AND ABOVE

The entire day he had been in the final throes of leaving his body. The death rattle was louder now in his chest as his lungs fought to breathe.

Kath called that evening.

Liz answered for me. The two sisters, like lions protecting their families.

'He is close now; his breathing has almost stopped. Do Sarah and the kids want to be here?'

Kath. Solid, reliable, kind and consistent. She was a rock. I had not seen her in the entire month as she had been at her brother's side the entire way to the end.

I walked closer to the fire.

I still couldn't talk and so Liz spoke for me. She was there. She was always there to help.

I considered the drive across town, the cold night. I closed my eyes and tapped into my own health.

I didn't want to be there.

I shook my head.

'Do you want to see Daddy and say goodbye?' I whispered to Ruby and Jude. Their eyes were wide. Both shook their heads.

'I am scared, Mom.'

I nodded. 'Me too.'

'They have said enough goodbyes, and this isn't necessary,' Liz agreed. 'They don't need to see him like that.'

I consulted with the Triumvirate via text.

'They are right. Let them lead,' the consensus came back.

Liz conveyed it. She talked quietly into the phone.

'No, Kath. She is not going to come. She's not up to it yet. Who is there with you?'

Everyone else was there, it seemed. She was, his mother and father, friends, family. Richard. The hospital was so full of his friends and family, all there to support him on this final passage, that they were

One last goodbye

spilling all over the corridors and in the canteen.

Friends had flown from out of town, and driven in. Random friends, and close friends. They all wanted to be there with him.

I walked through and into Ruby's room.

'Come sit by the fire with me,' I said. 'Daddy is going to be leaving soon so let's sit together.'

She followed me out of the room, rubbing her eyes. She hadn't been sleeping yet – it was just before 8 pm, and she was just on the edge of sleep. I left Jude to sleep, not entirely sure why.

I texted my sister Jayne, who was living in the cottage on my property, to come up and sit with us. My mom was there already with me, and my dad joined.

We all sat by the fire, and I sank into a low seat. We were all silent. Waiting. Dreading.

Jayne lit a candle.

At 8 pm the phone rang. It was Kath.

'He is gone.'

No noise. We just sat starting into the flame.

It is done. He is dead.

I send Vicky, Lulu and Georgia a text to tell them. The three sisters I have gathered in my life. The ones I want to tell first. *He's gone.*

I feel calm. Quiet. Peaceful.

Everyone else left to do things and sort things out as the candle flickered. Ruby was put back to bed. I heard text messages come in.

Liz kept me updated on all the details. They were going to dress him in his favourite jeans and shoes. His father was going to collect them. These details were specific and important. There was talk about collecting his clothes and death certificates.

I sat still. Silent.

Listening.

Waiting.

I felt deep calm and peace come over me.

LOVE AND ABOVE

Where might he be right now? Was he soaring? Was he scared? Was he relieved?

Would he come here and say goodbye? Would I feel it?

I closed my eyes for a while, to see if I could feel his presence.

I knew he was soaring, fast and high and far away already.

Eventually it was time to get up, and I realised I couldn't. I was sitting on the floor, too low for my still-inactive muscles to lift me.

Please help me stand up, I had to text.

Overcoat

*Not what I knew him well,
or could consider his wispy blonde hair
and overcoat part of my mental furniture,*

*We lunched now and then,
had impromptu suppers of grilled chops and salad,
while our kids ricocheted into a Friday evening.*

*We drank Pinotage, compared the notes Fatherhood brings,
spoke of our sons, and contemplated the years ahead
like a day up the coast.*

*We hardly spoke of the sinkers he carried in his pocket,
but I could see the bulge,
and puzzled by his courage, I fingered my own pockets –
empty, except for a used tissue and biscuit crumbs
and all the while gravity tugged like a Terrier
at the stitching of his overcoat.*

*Months ambled by,
I heard that a bed had been moved, furniture shifted,
and he had abandoned chemo,
I meant to call him, and then sudden as a paper cut
I heard he was gone.*

LOVE AND ABOVE

But there's always that overcoat,
The lapels turned up against Winter
About to enter our kitchen on a Friday evening.

– A poem by Stephen Symons

Survival mode

It's been a month since the funeral I still have a huge open hole in my throat where my tracheotomy was. They don't sew it up, they simply tape it over with a sticky plastic cover that billows and puffs out as I breathe.

If you have ever watched a bullfrog, you will understand what I looked like.

'It's embarrassing, Mom,' Jude says. 'My friends think it's weird. You sound like Darth Vader.'

'I am your father,' I rasp. Ooooops. 'Okay, maybe that was wrong timing,' I snicker.

I texted instead of talking.

My body is such a fragile and delicate thing that the smaller problems have gone unnoticed. Breathing is the bigger thing in the scheme of importance. My daily sessions with the physiotherapist in the hospital have been downgraded to weekly sessions as my lungs start to breathe more easily.

I am getting out of the bath one day when I look in the mirror to see a livid red thing running from my butt down to my knees. I freeze in the mirror. My brain is starting to slowly piece things together. Strange, itchy feeling down the back of my legs. I have thrush running all the way down my legs from the feeding tubes.

I am covered in scars.

I am thin. 'Being thin' has always been some dream. Not the deepest dream, I will confess. I was more interested in being athletic, fast and strong. But what girl doesn't look at those models wearing fantastic creations and want to look like that?

I hate the way I look, and I hate the way it feels.

LOVE AND ABOVE

Because thin means sick.

Thin wasn't losing the soft fat that made me curvy or gentle to touch. It wasn't just the small rolls around my middle or the few inches too many around my arms.

Thin has meant losing everything.

The primary reason is that I have no muscles left at all.

What happens in a coma, doctors explained, is that your body starts to cannibalise itself. It is the process banters aim to achieve. Ketosis: when your body has no food to draw on to stay alive and working, so it starts to use what it can find.

It starts with the fat supplies, but they don't last very long. So next it turns the best source of protein around – muscles – and it eats them. Added to that, muscles require continual use to maintain strength and size, and being still for long periods means they atrophy.

It isn't just my thighs that have gone; even the muscles that hold my bladder intact have gone. My fingers can't hold a pen.

Food. I am drowning in it. But I don't want to eat. It is hard to coordinate the actual chewing and swallowing of the food.

But added to that I'm not hungry at all. I have been fed on liquids for so long that food is scary.

'Just eat,' became the instruction.

All my emotional shields are down. I have almost lost my life. I have lost my husband.

I am totally broken. But instead of being broken up, I feel as if my heart is broken open, wide open, and that lets so much pour in.

I cried for him. I cried for myself. I cried everywhere, relentlessly and in front of everyone. Jude hates it so I slowly learn to find appropriate places and times.

When my eyes water he gives me The Look.

'Don't you dare cry again, Mom,' he says.

All my hair has fallen out. It started shedding, then coming out in handfuls. On my 38th birthday my girlfriends came for tea, took one

Survival mode

look at me and marched me to the hairdresser, who cut it all off.

I obsess about every second of his last few days. I pore over every photo taken of him while I wasn't there. I quiz everyone.

What did he say?

Did he miss me?

Did he ask for me?

Did he love me?

I needed every single tiny, terrible detail.

I've told a few close people how we had met each other in the spirit world. I was still trying to stay in the physical world.

No matter how terrible I feel, how much I just want to stay in bed all day, I still have to get up at 6 am and pack the school lunchboxes.

I have been keeping my circle very small – me and the kids and close family and very close friends. My absolute priority has been giving them as much safety and security as I have been able to given them. But most times they just get on with life and it is full of normal things like school, friends, PlayStation.

They ask questions like:

Where is Dad's body?

What happens when you stop breathing?

Can I phone him?

What would happen if Dad suddenly phoned us?

Jude told me months later that he thinks we are lying, that his dad is alive somewhere on a work trip and will come home still.

Reality will be a hard teacher.

I have battled to recover from the coma and the lung damage. From not being able to breathe or walk, I've had to learn to walk again on a Zimmer frame and physically recover from the illness. I was eventually put on steroids and my lungs have really improved. It is a long and slow healing process. I've spent months coughing up wads of phlegm that seem endless. My voice is coming back and the big hole in my throat is closing.

Post-traumatic bliss

I was carrying all my otherworldly secrets with me. Sometimes at night I would just close my eyes and feel myself shooting through the universe again. I would remember the Forest Man by my bed. I would feel the warm arms of the tribe of women and hear their songs.

And so I took a lot of time and wrote it all down, lest I forgot. As if I could.

As soon as I could hold a pen, I wrote it all down in notebooks.

I tried to make sense of what had happened to me physically.

I went back to visit my attending specialist physician for a check-up, and to quiz him on my medical records and what had happened.

'Sarah, your case was a medical anomaly,' he said. He pointed at a lung X-ray on the wall behind his desk.

'You see that X-ray? It is your lungs, and how they changed over a few hours from a speck to full coverage of infection. I have shown student after student and we have gone over it with the board, and it is just something we have never seen before.'

Before I left, he gave me my medical record to submit to the medical aid.

'What was the actual diagnosis?' I asked him.

'We are not even sure it was pneumonia,' he said. 'The final diagnosis was influenza – the flu.'

Next, I went down the hall to the ENT surgeon to see if I would get my voice back once the hole in my throat had closed. When he saw me, he did a double take and checked his chart again.

'Ms Bullen – were you the woman in bed A1?' he asked.

I had to check with my mom in the waiting room; she nodded.

Post-traumatic bliss

'You should not be alive,' he said. 'Do you know that I was called to resuscitate you when you had pulled out your tracheotomy? It was late at night and I wasn't at the hospital, and it took me a while to get there. By the time I got to you, you were royal blue and hadn't breathed for 24 minutes.'

He stood up and did a little hop and gave me a hug.

'Well done, young lady. This has made my day.'

I hadn't known that. I hadn't known anything. I promptly threw up in his bathroom.

I spoke to Murray for a long time about what had happened, both medically and on a soul level.

'At one point your sister Liz came to see me and told me how scared she was, that you would die too and that Ruby and Jude would lose you both. I knew that was not going to happen. I told her that the nature of life is going to take care of this. I knew that Llewelyn would die, but you would live.'

That week, Liz brought the kids home from school and stayed over and we sat chatting on my bed as we looked over the photos and the messages from around the world that were still pouring in.

She filled me in on some of the madness while I had been in the coma.

'People went crazy, Sarah – you were the cool, young, gorgeous family! You were known, loved and admired by huge circles across the globe. Suddenly, you were fighting for your life in a coma and Llewelyn was dying. Everyone wanted information and answers. We were bombarded.

'I stayed here at your house and totally took over. I kept the kids posted all the time. They really wanted to talk about what was going on and know the truth. They saw Llew every day. We talked so much about what happens when you die. Jude wanted details – what will happen if Mom and Dad both die? They wanted to know, and they needed to know. The school encouraged total honesty. Nothing could protect them from what was coming and not allowing them to be part of it would create fear and resentment.'

I told her more about my soul travels and we talked late into the night.

'Sarah, what the hell do you think actually happened?'

I told her about the ceremony with Llewelyn, and how I'd said goodbye to him.

'Do you think it was a karmic journey, a soul contract with Llewelyn? I think, sometimes, that the mind has such immense power over your body that you chose almost to go with him, rather than watch to him die.'

I nodded. 'It was all of those things, and it was also something beyond all reason and logic. It's hard for me to make sense of it yet, and I don't want to reduce it to a single message. I know that I have had such an easy ability all my life to connect to these realms, and I know that was what pulled me there. You know I have done this before, but the coma was the next level. I think I thought I could save him.'

We sat quietly for a long while.

'I do know that it ended up being my way of saying farewell to him. The other thing I do know is that I wanted to just float away. It is so strange, because that was not a conscious thought at all. I am the last person to ever think that. I have such a huge appetite for life. And at some point in the journey I made a very clear choice, and chose life.'

We combed through the Facebook threads and talked long into the night about souls and magic. We spoke about God and destiny.

'What I found in that spirit world is that we are guided in our lives. God was there. I don't really care what word you use for that power, but what I know is that there is something bigger than all of us and it is full of love.

'We all have a destiny in this journey of life, and mine was not to die then. I have some bigger journey still to live, Liz, and I am going to live a bit and find that path.'

Post-traumatic bliss

Friend after friend visited me. People I loved, and people I had never met. Colleagues I had worked with. They all wanted to come and see me. They sat in my lounge, held my hand and cried.

I was so grateful to see their pain. It was just that I wasn't feeling it.

'You are just numb right now.'

'Sometimes, after a long illness it is actually a relief. The pain will come.'

'You will get through this.'

'Give yourself time.'

'He is in a better place.'

I wanted to grieve. I wanted to feel. I *was* feeling. I was awash with feelings. But the feelings were different from those I expected to have.

They were:

Acceptance.

Delight.

Gratitude.

Love.

Grace.

Ecstasy.

Bliss.

Joy.

I was living in such a state of grace. I felt so blessed and connected.

I cried so much.

I felt so much.

I just didn't grieve.

Sure, I was also still fighting for my life. Coming off all the drugs meant I was paranoid, sleepless and scared. There were times I battled to breathe. There were nights when it got really hair-raising. On the steroids I would cough and hack until I retched and my lungs burned. I didn't want to be left alone. I was scared and fragile.

LOVE AND ABOVE

But my distinct lack of grief worried me the most.

It was hard to relate to the grief around me and the terrible shock. I simply could not be a part of it. I could barely look at his parents and see the pain in their eyes.

One phrase kept haunting me. So strange and foreign.

Have more fun.

The instruction that I was given by the Forest Man. It was an answer, a blessing and a message all at the same time. I just didn't know how to live it.

In fact, as the paranoia eased I felt the opposite of grief, and I was worried.

I went to see a psychologist and then also a trauma release specialist and counsellor, Julie Petrie.

'Sure, these emotions of grief are accurate for most people, but they don't come one after the other like steps on a ladder you climb to success. Any of these phases can come at any time. Some last for months, or minutes. And they can come back again and again,' she told me.

'Is it possible I am not grieving, that something is wrong with me? I am on a lot of medication. Do you think it is suppressing it?'

'Women like you have to hold families together, keep children's lives together. Bills have to be paid. Sometimes after a loss you are just trying to survive. If you need help from medication to do this, then take the help.'

She said that sometimes it takes years to start feeling safe enough to actually start processing what really happened. Most often, the first year is about just surviving. I was feeling that.

'We live in a new, death-denying, grief-dismissing world now. After an appropriate time, we must go back to work and pick up our life. We are told to find closure. We live in a productive society. Allow yourself time.'

Lulu and Georgia were there, day after day, to pull me through.

Post-traumatic bliss

'Sarah, you are done with all the stages of grief,' Lulu told me. 'I have watched you over the past four years and you have grieved. You are done.'

I nodded.

She took my hand.

'You are claiming your own right to live, my friend, and you nearly had to die to get there.'

I decided I wanted to come off all my medication.

'Absolutely do not do it,' Lulu told me. 'Sarah, you can't mess with this stuff, and you are not emotionally solid enough. Just a few months ago you were lying in a coma, about to die. Don't stop your meds yet. You will not cope and you will regress.'

'Stay on the meds,' Georgia said. 'Your kids need you to be present and calm.'

I stopped them anyway.

This was against the advice of the psychiatrist treating me, and the psychologist I saw once a week.

But it was my choice. It was as if my body just wanted to cut down.

I wanted so badly to feel it all. I didn't want to medicate it away, or soften it away, or dull it away. I wanted to feel every single emotion that came with being a human, being alive.

'You must be suffering from post-traumatic stress,' one visitor said. 'You and the kids.'

I was dumbfounded.

I wasn't. Not at all. I was so far away from that.

I thought I might be suffering from post-traumatic bliss instead.

Is there a condition where a life trauma cracks your heart open so wide that the entire universe can enter it?

Paging through my notebooks, I found a quote that was to mean so much to me over the recovery years. It was by the Roman general Marcus Aurelius.

LOVE AND ABOVE

'There is nothing that can ever happen to you that is not in the realm of human experience.'

This is it. I knew.

This is what it means to be human. The joy and the fun. The fear and the pain. All of it is part of the journey.

Love and above

All these secrets were making my world feel special and full of grace and magic. I was floating on grace and simply riding on the sheer joy of being alive.

We were all very busy with other stuff. A death seemed bigger, and that's what everyone wanted to talk about.

But I remembered.

I remembered the circle of dark and sweet women holding me.

I remembered soaring in the universe.

I remembered being a shining spear of light.

I remembered the Forest Man kissing me on the head and whispering the words to me.

Have. More. Fun.

So here I was, back here in this body and fully alive, but I couldn't forget the rest of the experience, nor dismiss it. I didn't want to.

I couldn't always hold on to the feeling; it was as slippery as sand running through my fingers. Often, I slipped back into the 'fear space', a space my brain knows intimately. Sometimes I call it anxiety or panic or terror. Fear as an emotion is always available to me in various forms.

I had worked out ways and devices and systems over the years to manage it. Skirting close to death and encountering angels did not remove the quality of fear; it only removed the fear of dying. And I could feel fear more clearly, and differently.

One night I woke up coughing, alone in the dead of night. I was back in that room, in that world of nightmares where I was dying. Cold sweat was making me shiver.

I sat up in my bed and turned on the bedside light to remind

LOVE AND ABOVE

myself who and where I was.

It was 2 am and I was terrified. I could feel the fear vibrate in my body. I sat with it for a while and let it rip through me, a tangible vibration of every cell.

Fear again. My old friend. Over so many years I had controlled it, disguised it, managed it and, if all else had failed, I had medicated it.

But again, the question came up: what are you actually afraid of? What is this terrible, uncontrollable fear racing through my body about?

I knew I was not afraid of death. I had been there, played there, and I knew there was nothing to fear. Just peace.

And I knew in that second that my enemy was fear. Not death. Not loss. Not illness. Not cancer. The real enemy was fear, and I could feel it vibrating through me. I could literally close my eyes and feel every cell in my body vibrating. It had a resonance and a frequency.

Then I moved my thoughts elsewhere. I remembered crawling out of that steam in the bush with the wild sky above me. My entire body had vibrated then, too.

Was it so different?

Yes, it was. As I flicked between the feelings, I could sense the vibration change. But could I change it and control it?

And it was then – sitting in the dark of night, alone in my room – that I made a startling choice: I will not be scared.

I am not scared.

It was a lightbulb moment.

It is one thing to think 'I will not be afraid', but how do you live it? For many months an answer had been stuck in my head and the words were crystal clear.

Have more fun

That was the key. Fun. Delight. Bliss. Joy. Rapture.

These were what would change fear into love.

I started to look more deeply at fear. I had listened to channelled

Love and above

teaching from Abraham Hicks for many years in my twenties, and studied metaphysics, so I went back to that. I joined the Krishnamurti Foundation and listened to all his talks on fear. He says, so many times, 'It really requires a great deal of enquiry as it is so subtle, so varied, so abstract. But is so real too.'

I read David Hawkins' *Power vs. Force*. Hawkins created what he called the Map of Consciousness. Simply put, he devised a scale that rates the energy level of basic human emotions, on a scale of 1 to 1 000. Any emotion rated below 200 is considered unhealthy for the individual and society, and anything above 200 moves into positive territory. From low to high, the levels of consciousness are: shame (20), guilt (30), apathy (50), grief (75), fear (100), desire (125), anger (150), pride (175), courage (200), neutrality (250), willingness (310), acceptance (350), reason (400), love (500), joy (540), peace (600) and enlightenment (700–1 000).

He conducted this research using kinesiology, or muscle testing, which seemed like an inexact science to me. However, I did know that fear had a vibration, and that it was very different from love. Of course, enlightenment is the space of Krishna, Buddha, Jesus, Mother Teresa.

All thoughts and emotions have their own vibrational frequency, or wave frequency, and quantum mechanics has demonstrated how a wave frequency can be altered. We can pop in and out of different levels at various times; usually, there's a comfortable resting state for most of us.

I knew mine had been fear and anxiety, and I was tired of it.

I knew fear was physical. I had felt it.

I knew love and joy and rapture had a feeling too.

I loved a practical solution and so, in my year of healing, I worked hard on playing with fear. Doing this told me that all emotions have a vibration that you feel in your body, and that fear is on the lowest end of the scale. To get rid of it, you have to raise it to a higher vibration, like love, gratitude or joy. You do this by crowding out fear-based thought

LOVE AND ABOVE

and replacing it with better thoughts. You choose love over fear.

I needed a practical solution like this. I can't think my way out of fear; I need to act my way out of it.

Get rid of fear by replacing it with love.

In four other simple words: Choose love and above.

I had been watching this phrase from afar for a while. I had even written it above my desk.

Now, there were two mantras next to each other: *Have more fun. Choose love and above.*

The message was getting louder now.

I listened to talks on love and gratitude. I downloaded meditations that planted positive thoughts in my mind. I stuck up affirmations and statements. I did a gratitude journal.

I tried to get back in touch with the people I had met in the spirit worlds during the coma. Where was the Forest Man and the tribe of beautiful women?

I started meditating for up to an hour a day. I was sucking up all the 'older wisdom' I could find. I took my hiyas out of the cupboard and dusted them off. I went to see Niall and we sat for a long time and spoke.

Much later, I joined a workshop he was running, and in it I created and built my own shrine with branches and ribbons. Niall came and gave me a clay pot to base it in and we prayed over it.

Every morning I did a pahla. I put on my hiya, knelt on the floor and spoke out loud all the things I was calling for. I called for grace and joy and love.

I called for forgiveness.

Have more fun.

The vow

I wasn't entirely sure yet how to find fun or bliss yet, but I made a vow. In fact, I made myself three very clear promises.
1. Say yes to the adventure.
2. Life is too short to ever wear black again.
3. Chase down joy and love.

Then I added a fourth:

4. Be celibate for a year.

I knew I needed this last one. Somehow, I knew the love and joy I was chasing was not going to be with another person.

Part 4

Greek island life

The summer of sannyasins

'It's a meditation centre and the perfect place to just wind down after this frenzy. There will be daily yoga and groups. Think about it . . . hot Greece in summer! Let's go there rather, and get out of Cannes?'

We were in Cannes at the annual film festival and it was all getting too hot and too much. Liz and I were sharing a room while she networked and partied as part of her marketing efforts for her film production company. It was eight months after I had got out of hospital and many commentators thought this trip to France was a step too soon.

I was starting to feel that too as the crowds and the world crowded in.

I was still thin as a reed, fragile and frail.

'What meditation? It is the Osho Centre?' I asked.

'Yes, and most of my friends are there. You will love it.'

Adventure. That was aligned with my vows and my search.

'I am in. Do we need to buy the maroon robes?' I asked.

Liz shook her head and logged on to Ryanair to find us a cheap flight to Athens.

'Not in Greece. It's only really in Pune that we wear the robes. But in Greece you can wear anything – or nothing. It's an olive farm and its mid-summer so the less we wear the better.'

The destination was Afroz, the Osho Meditation Centre on the small Greek island of Lesbos. Liz had been an Osho sannyasin (devotee) for close on seven years now, and I had read some of Osho's books and done many of his meditations before. A few years before, Liz had brought a facilitator out to Cape Town and we had done an

LOVE AND ABOVE

art as meditation process. I loved anyone who shared deep and old wisdom, and I took what I could from any religion. They all hold some truths.

Osho, born Rajneesh, was particularly interesting. He was an Indian spiritual teacher, guru and professor of philosophy who died in the nineties. He was highly unconventional and one of the first eastern gurus to speak about modern psychotherapy.

Osho was a controversial figure no matter which way you looked at it, and still is, decades after his death. He became famous for his book *Sex Matters: From sex to superconsciousness*. In reality, it was about moving one's consciousness from the first to the seventh chakra, but people went crazy for him as the 'sex guru'.

He travelled throughout India and lectured during the sixties, promoting meditation and the ideals of free love. He saw marriage as a form of social bondage, especially for women – which was highly controversial in India. His teachings repeatedly put him in conflict with Indian authorities and in the eighties he fell foul of the west, too, mostly due to his ill-fated decision to relocate with thousands of his followers to a commune in Oregon. At this time, Rajneesh adopted the title Bhagwan Shree Rajneesh. This part of his life was later captured in a Netflix documentary, *Wild Wild Country*.

When that failed, he fled back to India, where lived out his last few years and died in 1990. When he was kicked out of the USA, the media called him the most dangerous man alive and no country would even let his private jet land on their soil. It seemed a strange title for a guru propagating freedom of the individual and a higher consciousness.

Many people thought it a cult, and I must confess that thought had crossed my mind in the years I had watched Liz travel for months each summer to India. But we are very quick to label or dismiss things we don't understand.

In the eastern world, gurus are accepted teachers and Osho has endured. In fact, his teachings have reached so far beyond his own life

The summer of sannyasins

that there are still millions of sannyasins across the world, and you can find an Osho Centre in almost every country – even China, where everything is banned.

And so it was to one of these we were heading. To a summer of sannyasins and meditation and dance.

I had seen photos of Liz over the years in Pune and had long coveted the maroon robes and bikinis worn by all sannyasins there.

An hour later, we had stuffed our cocktail dresses and high heels into suitcases and were sitting on a bus back to the Cannes – Mandelieu Airport to zip across to Athens before we connected via the small Aegean flight to the capital of Lesbos, Mytilene.

When we landed on the small island and I took my first deep breath of the sweet warm air, it was intoxicating.

The light captivated me, the colour and the sounds. But mostly it was the light and the quality of the air. In Africa we say this is where the ancestors live – in air, the ether. The ethereal realm. Not real and tangible, but all around anyway.

The Greek air spoke to my soul.

I felt shivers down my spine. I felt it before in my early twenties when I'd travelled here. It called to me. I know this place. I know this air.

The first glimpse of a holiday with a difference was the sign at Mytilene Airport, *Welcome Lesbians*, flapping in the hot island wind. But I was swallowed up in the sweaty mix of families welcoming friends and tourists trying to find a cab. The plan was to spend ten days at a meditation resort just outside a small coastal village.

Adonis, the taxi driver, explained it on the way: 'We are all lesbians here!' he chuckled. 'I am proud to say I am a lesbian.'

We arrived at the centre and were shown across the olive farm to a small stone cottage with two beds, a shower and a toilet. Perfect. A few of these cottages were nestled in the open expanse of land, some under green-grey olive trees.

LOVE AND ABOVE

We unpacked; the sticky heat of summer hit us and we fell down into a dead afternoon sleep.

Later that afternoon, in a post-siesta daze, we stumbled out of the cottage as flute music snaked through the olive trees and over the warm air towards us.

'You need to wear white,' Liz told me as, back inside, we flung clothes on the bed to find something suitable. 'It's the Evening Meeting, or White Robe Ceremony. We must attend. This happens every night in Osho centres all over the world and we all have to wear white. It's not a strict here, but in Pune there are white robes.'

She pulled a sheer, white, lacy dress out of her bag and paired it with some shorts and a bikini top. I scrambled through my colourful wardrobe for anything white, finding only a long cotton dressing gown. The no-black rule had almost ruled out white too.

'Perfect,' she laughed. 'Pop a bikini under it.'

I slid some shorts on and a tank top, snickering as if we were going to a costume party.

As we neared the clearing, I realised anything – or nothing – would have been suitable.

An expansive white marble floor rose in the open air from the ground and figures dressed in white were swaying to the music, arms in the air.

Lithe, lean and lush women in bikinis. Others in long flowing skirts. There were men in long cotton pants, some in sarongs. Others in swimming trunks only, their bodies glistening in the late afternoon heat.

The music pulled us closer and a small crowd gathered around Liz as they saw her.

'Zuri,' they murmured, pulling her into a tight hug. One by one they embraced her, each one a long hug. I saw that this was truly her tribe. Here, with these easy and beautiful people, she was at home.

They turned to me. I stood there, thin and scared, my hair shorn,

The summer of sannyasins

a long cotton dressing gown skirt half falling off me. I knew nobody. I grinned broadly.

They pulled me into a huge embrace. Each person I met grabbed me and pulled me in. Deva. Shakti. Abhijeet, Mridu, Swargo, Vikalpo. Nirdosh. Adiraj. Gulistan, Zikr.

Names I tried to wrap my tongue around.

I had known that she was called Zuri in this world, and finally I saw her. Her hair long and flowing down her back, she weaved and danced. I had watched my sister on so many dancefloors over the years, but this one was the best. Her body moved gently to the music and her face shone with love.

I moved into the space and joined them, my feet sliding on the marble and my arms high in the sky.

The music grew as we moved faster and faster through the Buddha Grove. Swirling and jumping.

Later that night we called a series of taxis and drove the ten minutes down the hill to the beach. We tumbled out and into the small Greek seaside village of Skala Eressos.

A small grocer beckoned me, with fresh red cherries spilling out.

'Come, let's go dance!' Zikr and Zuri pulled me onwards with the crowd. We headed to Zorba the Buddha, a cocktail bar that was perched dangerously on a deck right over the Aegean Sea.

Lean bodies were dancing to the house music. Spanish, Greek, Turkish, Italian, American.

I sat back with a cocktail, watching.

'What's with all the strange names everyone has?' I asked. 'It is so hard to remember them all.'

'We have all taken sannyas and when we do that we let go of our given names,' Zikr explained, her native Spanish tongue rolling the words. 'Sannyas is one of the four ashrams or stages of life in Hindu philosophy. Those who adopt it often give up all possessions and drift from one place to another, with no worldly possessions and

LOVE AND ABOVE

no emotional ties.

'Of course, it is not so strict in the Osho world. He called it neo-sannyas and said it simply means the movement of the seekers of truth. He also says you can move in and out of it, like your sister does as she moves into her job.'

She nodded at Liz.

'She cannot be Zuri back there. There she must be Elizabeth and so she moves in and out as it suits her.'

A number of women were walking past, holding hands.

'There *are* a lot of women here,' I mused.

'I think maybe it's a women's festival,' Liz nodded. 'I didn't notice so many last time.'

We glanced over at the bar just down the strip. All women.

A lot of women were dancing together.

A lot of them were kissing.

We looked at each other and nodded.

'I think that sign at the airport was for real,' I said.

We both laughed.

'Didn't you know?' Zikr asked as she laughed with us. Tears were streaming down our cheeks.

'This village is the capital of lesbianism in the whole world. All people are welcome here. Greeks. Gays. Lesbians. Lovers. Meditators. This place is freeeeeeedom. It is love. You are so welcome, beloved.'

Her arms went in the air as she danced across the floor.

One woman, who'd lived almost three thousand years ago, was the siren who called women and poets to this island. Sappho. Not much was really know about her and huge debates raged among classicists and historians about her life, her work, her sexuality and her family. She was reportedly born on the island in about 600 BC. Many languages use the island's name for describing the love two women have for each other. She was credited with a four-line stanza form called the Sapphic stanza.

The summer of sannyasins

Some of the islanders of Lesbos had taken offence and started a court case to reclaim the word 'lesbian'. They demanded that Greek courts ban its use to describe gay women. It was the source of much amusement in the lesbian bars on the island, I was to find out.

Sappho's name and her fragments of verses have endured through the ages. She was the muse of writers and poets, and her name still called women every summer to visit the island.

Her name caught in my throat as Zikr moved away into the night.

I leaned back and looked around.

This was it.

The place I had been looking for without even knowing it. The place I had tried to touch.

This was so far from the fear and the terror of the world of nightmares. It was light and bliss and fun.

This was joy.

This was fun.

This was pure delight.

It wasn't just the place . . . it was the feeling and the energy of the people.

I knew it wouldn't last forever, but I could feel it. And I wanted to stay with that feeling.

The words I had woken with a year ago, and the mantra burned into my brain and written on my wall, started to activate on some level. They were just words before.

Have. More. Fun.

Love and above.

Yes. It was time.

I was in just the right place.

And I knew just the person to do it with. He found me the next morning at breakfast.

Wild, wild country

The open-air kitchen and dining hall was rigged so that everyone washed their own dishes. Huge serving tables were laden with food grown in the fields. Bowls of olives and cucumbers were stacked high. Fresh dark bread had been delivered that morning from the village bakery, there was a bowl of boiled eggs and a platter of juicy Greek tomatoes. Of course, there was essential olive oil at every table. I piled my plate high with the exotic food.

I was not well travelled and not quite sure how to put it all together, so I watched a few people first.

They sliced the tomatoes into quarters, added thick chunks of cucumber and slabs of feta. A salad for breakfast? This was news to me.

I put mine on a slice of the bread and closed my eyes in delight as I bit into it. Juicy tomato ran down my chin, mingling with salt and olive oil.

I had spotted Swaram during breakfast and had watched him. He was short and dark, with deep-set moody eyes and thick curly black hair. It curled down his back. He had a strong, bent nose, the kind I found so intriguing. He looked kind and real.

He slipped onto the bench next to me and ran his hands over my short hair and down my neck.

'I like this,' he said as his fingers went through my hair. 'Verrrrry sexy.'

His thick Greek accent made my stomach tighten.

I smiled, wiping the juice away and taking another bite.

'Sarah – and you are?'

Wild, wild country

'Swaram. Are you staying the summer, Zara?'

I shook my head. 'No, I am just here for ten days. You stay the whole summer?'

He nodded. 'I do every year. I stay four months. Pity you are leaving. I saw you arrive last night with Zuri. She is my friend.'

'She's my sister,' I said.

'Ah. So different. You are . . . longer, ναί?' He was looking for the English words.

Then he took my hand and pulled me up.

'I am joining a meditation group now. It's called No Mind and it runs for seven days. Why don't you come and then we can walk down to the beach, and I can show you the land where we are planting the vegetables?'

I nodded and gulped down my black coffee.

'Sure, that sounds fun. Let's do it.'

Ten minutes later I walked into the meditation room. The doors closed and about twenty of us were there to begin.

The instructor, Anekant, explained what was going to happen. 'Osho No Mind Meditation is a process of one hour of gibberish and then one hour silence. For the first hour you will talk gibberish. For the next hour you will sit in silence as you let go, lie down and go deeper into the centre of your being.'

I grinned. Easy. This was going to be fun.

He was reading from an Osho book, *Meditation*, now: 'The word gibberish comes from a Sufi mystic Jabbar. Jabbar never spoke any language, he just uttered nonsense. Still he had thousands of disciples . . .'

I looked at Swaram and smiled, but he was deep in thought. Or meditation? I wasn't sure, but his eyes were closed as he stood in the middle of the room, his hands in a mudra position.

His hair was loose, and it fell down his back in long waves. His baggy cotton pants were tied at the waist, and he wasn't wearing a shirt.

LOVE AND ABOVE

He must have pulled it off and thrown it down.

I was trying to concentrate on the instructions.

'Go consciously crazy. Standing or sitting, close your eyes and make any sound you like, but do not speak in a language, or use words that you know. Throw everything out. Go totally mad. Everything is allowed. Sing. Shout. Scream. Mumble. Talk. Let your body do whatever it wants to do. Jump. Sit. Lie Down. Kick. If you cannot find sounds just say la la la – but do not remain silent.'

Then a gong sounded, and the process started.

It sounded like a kindergarten class had been let out of school early. Twenty voices rose high, screaming and shouting a language all made up. Gibberish.

I stood stock still for a while, trying to orientate and make sense of this meditation. Then I shrugged, remembering my vows. This was adventure. I was willing and open-hearted. Let's do this.

I opened my mouth and let rip. People were pacing, stomping, crying. Clothes were coming off. Thins were being thrown and walls were being hit.

I joined in.

Hoi soooo lamamamay wahhoooo

I shouted and screamed. I sounded Italian. Then Chinese.

Then I started coughing. This wasn't a gentle cough. It was a deep, spasmodic and retching cough that was part of the healing process of my lungs. I knew this cough well because it happened up to five times a day. Once I started it didn't end until I had expelled a wad of phlegm. That sometimes meant me retching, gagging and falling to the floor.

It was the cause of much mortification for my kids.

'Pretend you don't know me,' I would gasp if this happened in public, which it did at least twice day. 'Walk away. Walk away now.'

Now I was in a crowded room and the cough started to crank up.

Luckily the room was so loud nobody heard. It seemed appropriate. It felt part of the process. But I knew it was going to end in

Wild, wild country

retching and I wanted to get out.

I would always extract myself from a room if this happened. But this door was closed. Was it locked?

I headed to it. It was open, and I staggered out into the hot air.

Finally, I could let it play out.

Cough. Cough. Retch. Cough. Cough.

The door opened and Swaram was looking out at me. He had a bottle of water in his hand which he walked over and gave to me.

I snatched it and gulped some down. That could often stop a coughing fit. It was as if the diaphragm movement of a swallow could break the spasm. This time it did not.

'Come back in,' he said.

I nodded and waved him back into the room.

'Inhaled something,' I gasped. 'Totally fine – leave me.'

I flapped my hand and he laughed and closed the door.

Once I had got it under control, I smoothed down my hair and went back into the room.

Nobody had noticed. In fact, there were other people in similar states of physical expression. One girl in a bikini was writing on the floor, beating her fists. A man was roaring and choking with sobs as he screamed.

Anekant walked up to me and put a hand on my shoulder.

'Take it easy,' he smiled.

This time I didn't put in a hundred per cent effort like I usually did. I didn't have to be the loudest and the wildest in the room. This room was even wilder.

I could just put in some gentle effort.

I was exhausted. I was standing in the corner and panting from the effort of speaking. I slowed down and looked around the room. People of all ages were in this space, totally unself-conscious.

I hadn't spoken much in the past eight months. In fact, I had only started speaking about three months after I'd got out, and the sheer physical effort of pushing air out of my lungs and up and over my vocal cords was draining.

Then, cutting through the roars and screams, the gong sounded. Not a moment too soon.

Instantly the room fell silent. Everyone moved slowly to get a meditation stool or seat and sit down on the wooden floor.

'Witness,' said the facilitator. 'Sit absolutely still and silent and relaxed. Gather your energy inwards, let your thoughts drift further and further away from you. Allow yourself to fall into the deep silence and peacefulness that is at your centre.'

I found a spot where the sun was streaming in and sat against the warm wall.

'Be aware. Be totally in the present moment. Become like a watcher on the hills, witnessing whatever passes by. Don't judge them. Don't get caught up in them. What you are watching is not important, it is the process of watching. Remember not to become identified with what comes by. Let them pass.

Thoughts.

Feelings.

Sensations.

Body.

Judgements.

Let them pass by.'

I sat there in the morning sun with my eyes closed and I knew I had found a key to the answers I was seeking. All the little pieces I had been holding were all coming together.

I had been running from fear, trying so hard to outwit it. Now, I could just watch it. I sat very still and very alert, knowing I was watching something change inside me.

I felt the air change in the room and I knew he was behind me. The Forest Man. My spirit guide. An angel? I was no longer sure what name to use.

Wild, wild country

I felt him smile and I felt his warm hands on my shoulders.

Tears streamed down my face. Inside me I felt the cells vibrating. It was not fear at all. It was love. Pure love and joy and delight. I could feel it.

I wanted to stay there forever, and I barely heard the next gong.

Everyone was slowly and quietly lying down. I moved like a ghost, filled with light and peace, not wanting to lose the feeling.

'Gibberish is dumping out the active mind. Silence is to get rid of the inactive mind. Now, you enter the transcendental. When you throw out the mind and all its activity, you remain – pure, clean, transparent and perceptive.'

I lay on the floor and remembered lying on other floors, or places, feeling this. I remembered lying down outside the sweat lodge at Phakalane. I remembered crawling out of the prayer hut in Botswana and lying down, looking at the stars above me.

Bliss.

Rapture.

Connection.

No room for fear here.

The meditation ended in a final gong, and then silence. I walked out into the sun. I may have floated. I felt as if I was walking on air.

Swaram grabbed my hand.

'Let's go to the beach,' he grinned. 'Grab some walking shoes. We are going to walk if you are okay with that. It's a 45-minute walk each way and we can buy some lunch on the way back.'

He pulled me close into a tight hug. Ah, the delicious smell of his skin as it pressed against me, hot and steely. A thick mat of black hair covered his chest, which was wet with sweat, drenching my shirt.

It felt so simple and so right.

I laughed, but even as I did I could feel tears prick my eyes. How stupid; I blinked them away.

'Let's forget our troubles together,' he said.

LOVE AND ABOVE

Then he leaned forward and kissed me gently. Just a light and delicious kiss and his tongue touched mine, warm and welcomed.

Yes, my soul screamed.

Yes to joy.

Yes to kisses.

Yes to adventure.

Yes to new experiences and wild joy.

Yes to life.

Yes to it all.

'Let me grab my bag and a hat,' I told him. 'I want to see if Liz . . . erm . . . Zuri will join us.'

'Don't worry about your swimsuit,' he called after me. 'We are going to the Sahara. The naked beach.'

My stomach lurched and I almost tripped.

'You are joking?' I squealed.

'No joking. Why? Yatee? You not like naked?

This was all happening so fast. So crazy. There was going to be nowhere I could hide with my short hair, skinny frame and scars.

Holy crap.

I ran my fingers through my hair self-consciously.

'I do like,' I said, gulping.

A crowd joined us on the walk down to the beach and we all laughed and sang as we passed the winding roads and small shepherds' huts and olive groves. I put my shades on. It wasn't for the sun; it was to hide the tears I could not stop flowing down my face.

The hot tears flowing were not sadness.

They were joy.

Love.

Being alive.

This.

Something was happening to me. I was finding the way to finally live the glimpses I had seen in my soul travels. I was starting to see that

Wild, wild country

fun was it. It was the answer, and the passport to joy.

It was so hot by the time we got to the beach that we all just stripped off instantly and ran into the crystal sea.

The beach was vast and empty with black sand like a scalding path of pain as we ran back to our bags and sarongs. I rolled in it, feeling the hot black grains stick to my wet skin.

All the bodies were naked and glorious. Other bathers lay on the beach, or swam in the ocean. All naked and free. The size or shape did not matter, nor did the gender or form.

He lay in the sun next to me and traced a long slow path down my back with his finger.

'Tonight,' he said. 'After dinner and dancing I give you massage. You like tantra?'

I smiled lazily at him.

'I do now,' I said.

Seduced into the love of life

Two weeks in Greece wasn't enough, and the deep feeling of connection I had found in the silence of the No Mind Meditation stayed with me.

When I landed back in Cape Town it was winter and cold, wet and grey. I slumped into my house and pulled my heavy suitcase up the stairs and into my lounge. I was back. I sat down heavily on the couch and looked around.

Same house. Same bed. Same car.

I didn't belong here, in this sameness, any more.

That weekend I sat at dinner listening to my friends chatting. All their husbands were there and the wine was flowing.

I stood up abruptly and drove home. I got into bed and read my diary, where I had a quote I had noted down: *I am here to seduce you into a love of life; to help you to become a little more poetic; to help you die to the mundane and to the ordinary so that the extraordinary explodes in your life. – Bhagwan Shree Rajneesh (Osho)*

I called Liz. She was in Greece for the entire summer and had moved out of the Osho Centre now and rented a small cottage up the road.

'What are you doing now?' I asked, longing in my voice.

I heard her laugh and other voices, muffled, came across the air.

'We're in a taxi. It is so hot here we are going to the Sahara beach for a late-night swim.'

I lay back and looked at the white ceiling.

'Liz, should I come back?'

There was a long silence.

'Don't you have a magazine deadline?' she asked.

Seduced into the love of life

'I do, but I can work from there, I guess.'

'Who will look after the kids?'

'Mom will stay with them.'

Another pause.

'If you think they will be okay, then come.'

That night, I booked a ticket back to Greece.

People raised eyebrows.

'What about the kids? You can't possibly leave them again.'

'I am,' I said.

So, it was a week later that I got back on the plane to Athens. I was going back to the Summer Festival.

Hundreds of spiritual seekers from all over the world had found their way to this small Greek island for ten days of madness and magic. Tents were put up all over the farm and beautiful people danced through the evening light. Men, women, children mixed with goddesses and gods. The festival started with the White Robe Ceremony, and it was as if ancient gods had sent all their muses, all the earth, for this.

Beautiful women in flowing robes swayed and danced through the trees, lanky men of all shapes and sizes writhed and laughed. Bodies were moving, fit and healthy and full of love. I was drawn to the magic, like a moth to a flame.

The Osho Centre was fully booked but Liz was staying at a farm just up the road.

'Share with me,' she said.

That night I stood in my white skirt and shirt in the centre of the Buddha field and cried with joy. This was it. This.

We danced and sang till the music stopped.

Liz and I got back to the house and took a cold shower out under the stars before we crawled into the bed. In the middle of the night, I got up to close the window.

I fell straight through the floorboards of the loft and onto the floor below.

LOVE AND ABOVE

'What the fuck!' Liz was running towards me. She was screaming. I was screaming.

I was lying over a staircase sideways, gasping. I had landed on the railing of the staircase. Correction: it wasn't a floor I had fallen through. The owner had simply covered the floor with a polystyrene board.

He came charging up the stairs. The sound of me hitting the staircase had been loud.

'Ela! Ela!' he was shouting. 'My God. My God! What did you do? What did you do? Did you not hear me tell you not to walk there?' His hands were in the air.

I did recall he had told me that as I had briefly dropped my bags off earlier. But that was before a few tequilas and a lot of holotropic breathwork.

I did a body scan. Liz was frantic.

'I think I'm okay,' I told her as I crawled over the balustrade and onto solid ground. I went back up the stairs to the loft. I was sore. So sore.

'Look. Kita – I put this chair here. Right here. To stop you walking. Why you walk there? Why?'

Yes, that was the chair I had moved in my sleepy state to get to the window.

'I am fine,' I gasped. I wasn't entirely sure I was.

I crawled back into bed and went back to sleep.

When I woke the next morning I knew I had broken a rib, or two. The pain was severe as I breathed and moved.

'Let's get you to a doctor,' Liz said.

Agony. To move. To breathe. We walked the mile down the road to the Osho Centre. It was 9 am and the sun was already tracking across the sky. The road was humming with the warming sands and the goats were heading out to the fields.

The walk along the ancient roads down the hill was the longest

Seduced into the love of life

and slowest I had taken in a year. I was wincing as I walked, and each movement twinged my ribs. We snagged a coffee from the open kitchen and waited. Zuri went to the morning Vipassana as I sat outside the office waiting for the doctor to finish his breakfast.

The doctor at the Osho Centre examined me and declared it.

Broken ribs.

'Ti pota. Nothing. There is nothing we can do,' he told me, shrugging.

'What about painkillers?' I suggested, practically.

He nodded and wrote a script. I called a taxi to the village and Liz and I waited in the baking sun on the street to catch our ride. As we neared the village I glanced at the script. Paracetamol. I balled the script in my fist.

'C'mon,' I said. 'You are kidding me. These are for a mild fever. These aren't for the level of pain I am in.'

I turned to Liz, who was vastly relieved it was just a broken bone. She had tears in her eyes.

'Sarah, I really don't know if I can take another thing going wrong,' she said.

I put my hand on her arm. 'I am so sorry. I know how much you have been through, Liz,' I told her. Tears sprung into my eyes too. 'I wish this hadn't happened.'

She took my hand. 'Sarah, no. It wasn't your fault. I could have done the same thing, anyone could have. It was the most stupid and unsafe thing ever. I am just sorry it happened to you. It is the last thing you need right now.'

'The ribs are nothing. I mean, I am sorry for everything, Liz. Me. Llew. I am not sure how it all went so wrong.'

She nodded.

We sat back against the sticky plastic seats and held hands as we careened down the mountain to the small apothiki (pharmacy). The Osho Centre was high on the dry hills, under the cooler balm of an olive grove. But step out and the hot tar strip down to the beach town was a stretch of rising heat.

As we turned the corner towards the beach village, the small settlements got denser. This was no tourist paradise, waiting for a ferry to land. Skala Eressos was hard to find and, once you were there, a hidden jewel. A bohemian village of lesbians and meditators.

Most Greek villages had two different settlements serving the same population. One was the 'winter village', which was higher up in the mountains. But in the heat of the summer the inhabitants relocated, moving down to the beach town that was cooled by the sea and the winds. Many villagers owned a summer house at the beach, and a winter house in the village. The winter village was called Eressos, and its summer counterpart, just four kilometres down the hill, was called Skala Eressos. 'Skala' meant 'ladder', but it might as well have meant 'beach'.

Routhena at the apothiki never smiled, and when I slipped her the script she looked at my face and shook her head. I was holding my side, wincing as I walked.

'Pain?' she asked. 'Too bad.'

I nodded. She looked down at the scribbled script and shook her head. Then she turned and pulled a pack of 60 Myprodol off the shelf. I closed my eyes in relief.

'Try these. Stronger.'

I handed over the cash and dry-swallowed the first two. They made no difference.

Later that day, over lunch, I ordered a carafe of wine. I chugged down two more painkillers. Zuri raised her eyebrows.

'Is that wise to mix all those?'

I laughed. 'Probably not!'

Half an hour later I could breathe and move again for the first time since the floor had opened up beneath me. Before I left the village and started the long walk back up to the farm, I slipped into the supermarket and bought a bottle of vodka.

'No way,' Zuri said as she saw me slip it into my backpack. 'That is going too far now. Are you mad? You can't mix that stuff.'

'I know it's not right, but it's taking the edge off the pain,' I countered. 'Look, I am not going to get addicted to these things.'

She raised an eyebrow.

'I don't know how else to get through this level of pain. If I get back home and the pain has gone and I am still mixing painkillers with alcohol, then I will address it. But for now, I am calling this my lifeline.'

That night was the opening night of the festival and I wanted to be there, dancing into the dark night. We went back to the small cottage and had a late-afternoon siesta. As I walked into the loft room, I turned to the floor I had fallen through and stood, incredulous, starting at the polystyrene board.

Right there, in one corner, was a sizable hole, the one I had made as I stepped onto the treacherous surface. I didn't dare look down. At least three metres below was the floor, and the staircase that had broken my fall.

I wanted to put it all behind me. I was here to have fun, goddamit. I was here to sing and dance and kiss beautiful Greek men. I wasn't supposed to be inching my way down onto the mattress, half-feverish with pain as the late-afternoon heat sucked me down into a deep and painless sleep. But here I was.

When I woke my breath was ragged from pain. I chugged down two more pills, and this time I took a few big sips of vodka. I slipped the pack into my bag and got ready for the opening of the festival.

We walked down towards the farm as the gong sounded across the fields and farms. It shook the air with its call, the air that shimmered with excitement.

Swaram was there. I could see him as I walked into the Buddha Grove, and he smiled as he saw me.

As the music rose, we moved towards each other, dancing and

LOVE AND ABOVE

laughing. Our bodies touched and moved apart. I was gliding with joy and love, tinged with the glazed and dreamy eyes of a person with two broken ribs and blood full of painkillers and vodka.

I was here. Far away from the pain and the ordinary. I was here in Greece for the summer, and I was going to have this time, pain or none.

And I was not afraid of anything.

'Welcome back! Where are you staying, beautiful?' he laughed as we walked out later.

'Up the road.'

'You will stay with me tonight, no?'

I smiled and nodded. It was if no time had passed. No questions asked. We were not concerned about the mundane details of real life, or where I had been or if I had a husband at home. We were both there, and open to it.

Later that night, we walked back towards his cottage. I never wanted to go home. I couldn't find the joy or the love there. All I could find there were the memories, the pull of the ordinary, the routine and the conventional.

I knew I hadn't journeyed through worlds and come back from the dead to stay at home and safe. I hadn't come back to be tame.

I knew that life could change in a heartbeat and that I was creating a new story for myself. This one was full of joy and delight and bliss and fun.

It could all change in an instant again, but while it lasted I was going to wear colours and dance, I was going to laugh and chase adventures.

Pulling the kids out of school

It was raining in Cape Town, cold and driving rain, which reflected my mood. I was back. The Greek village had closed for the winter and all the colour and light had gone out of my life again.

I was late. Driving had been a hard skill to master after the coma and I often got lost. Small things were still missing and often my brain could still not multitask. Some basic cognitive skills were hard to regain. I could not recall names or faces. I had to learn to write and then type again. But most alarming was my short-term memory loss. I often couldn't find my car, or keys, or bag, or I would get confused and drive to the wrong house.

The first time I drove a car, I simply didn't turn at a hairpin bend. Fully loaded, I ramped straight over the pavement, popping two airbags and two tires.

I pulled up outside Camps Bay Preparatory School to collect Jude at least twenty minutes late that day. The school had been the family that had held the children the tightest. It was their safe haven, between friends, teachers and parents.

As I parked, I saw a small figure standing at the fence, waiting for me and watching. The rain was pelting down, streaming down his blonde hair.

I jumped out and ran to him. His face was white with terror, and the rain had mixed with his tears.

'Let's get you in the car,' I said, glancing at the aftercare teacher behind us, who gave me a look of desperation and a shrug.

'He was waiting for you. I told him to come inside but he was worried something had happened to you,' she told me. I held him very tight as I carried him away.

'What were you worried about?' I asked as I towelled him down and bundled him into the warm car. He didn't speak. His eyes were wide with terror.

'I guess that's a stupid question.'

I kept talking and holding him until he finally started breathing again. Then he started to sob.

'Don't die, Mommy. Please don't leave us alone.'

My heart felt as if it would break and shatter into a million little pieces. His sobs filled the car, the first time he had shown any emotion.

I turned on the heater as I drove. When we pulled up at home, I turned to him.

'Do you want to go to school?'

'No, I want to stay with you. I am scared there.'

'So here's the deal,' I told him. 'I refuse to let you go to school. You are staying at home with me. In fact, I will only agree that you can go back when you beg me, and you tell me you are so bored of me that you want to go back. Is that a deal?'

He held on to me like a limpet, his face so warm in my neck.

'Thank you, Mommy,' he said. 'I just want to stay with you.'

We lay that afternoon on the couch and read together in the sun.

Later that night I cooked dinner and the three of us sat around the fire and ate.

An idea had been brewing in my mind. It was not fully formed, but it was enough to go on.

'Ruby, Jude – how would you feel about us all going to live in Greece for a year?'

They both looked up at me, surprised.

'Is that where *Mamma Mia!* was?' Ruby asked.

I nodded.

Pulling the kids out of school

They both grinned.
'Yes, let's go!'
The spirit of adventure was calling us on.

Open the seven gates

I was going to answer adventure's call. I was going do something to blast away the old and open a door to the new.

None of us belonged in these same spaces or places any more. We had to find a new way and live into a new life. But there was something bigger going on than simply moving overseas and shaking things up. I knew on a fundamental level that if I wanted to change and grow, I had to start taking different actions. It would not happen if I kept everything the same.

I knew I had been through an initiation of fire and soul. I was being called to change and transform again.

I designed a personal process to guide me forward and light the way. I based it on a story that I often told in women's circles and writing groups, that of Inanna's descent into the underworld. Inanna was a huge and powerful goddess of the ancient Sumerians of Mesopotamia, in what is now Iraq. In mythology and writing, the road of trials of the hero's journey often requires entering the underworld or the land of the dead. In shamanic cultures, rituals of rebirth often require the initiate to enter a state of death to arise reborn.

Inanna's story has been told for centuries and was written in cuneiform, inscribed on clay tablets in the form of a poem.

Remember, the underworld is not hell, but rather a dreamy place, a different empire. Inanna was the Queen of Heaven, but that was not enough for her. There are many stories about her great feats, her lovers and her shepherd king Dumuzi. But the most enduring story of hers is when she chose to leave her entire kingdom behind to descend into the underworld to visit her sister Erishkagal, who had lost her husband

Open the seven gates

Gugalanna – the Bull of the Heavens.

Inanna abandoned heaven and earth to descend to the underworld.

She gave up all her worldly possession to do this.

All her temples and all her lands.

With the symbols of her power as a woman, and a queen and a god.

And with these things, this armour of a woman, her accomplishments, Inanna set out for the underworld.

As she journeyed there, she had to pass through seven successive gates. At each gate she was met by Neti, the gatekeeper of the underworld. At each gate, she was symbolically stripped of her power. First her crown, then her necklace, then her ring and staff. Willingly, she surrendered all she had accomplished in life until she was stripped naked as she entered the last room.

But when she entered, her sister struck her dead. Inanna was turned into a corpse, a piece of rotting meat, and was hung naked from a hook on the wall. For three days and three nights she hung there. Finally, the gods sent her the food and water of life to bring her back. She rose anew. A woman reborn.

The story of Inanna had long struck me as profound. It is the journey of death and rebirth. It is a journey of finding out what is transient, and what is eternal. It is a tale of initiation to find out our true calling and our most authentic selves.

This was such a critical story of initiation and transformation. Initiation is the place so many of us avoid. I wanted to move forwards. But I could see that this was not the solution. I couldn't just rush out of that holding place of the underworld. I wanted to emerge from it into the new myth I was creating.

I challenged myself to walk through seven gates in this process, each one forcing me to emerge as changed.

LOVE AND ABOVE

Gate 1: Embrace the in-between space

Sometimes, emptiness is not vacancy, but rather a long gestation. Gestation by the ego's measure is most often too long. But, by soul's measure, the length of the waiting and making within, before what is being created shows on the outside, is ever just right.
– Clarissa Pinkola Estés, *Untie the Strong Woman*

We want hard or difficult times to end, and when they do we don't notice.

This gate asks you to allow yourself to be in a waiting place, a time to embrace the unknown. This is the period in which you let go of everything you used to be, before the new beginnings.

This is the place where Inanna was willingly hanging on a hook as a corpse. It is unlikely it will be only three days and three nights. See this time for what it is, without wanting it to end, and allow the possibility of what you will step into and become next to emerge.

Gate 2: Allow great loss

We have to be willing let go of the life we planned so as to have the life that is waiting for us. – Joseph Campbell

We have to let things end, sometimes entire lives we imagined.

This gate asks you to find and release people, old vows, agreements or promises you may have made. It asks you to identify and take out the hooks that have been holding you to your old story.

I started to do very practical things. I systematically looked at and took back any the vows and agreements I had made that no longer served me or my new life. I sat quietly one night and sadly revoked my marriage vows. I had made them at 28, full of hope and love, but they were no longer part of my story so I burned them in the flames. I did it with love, but I had to release myself from them.

Open the seven gates

I revoked the vow of celibacy I had made and I carefully and reverently started to unhook the old from my life.

Release everyone and everything.

Gate 3: Enter the silence

Enter into silence and listen. This can be in meditation, a process or a choice.

This gate asks you to give up all the other voices that clutter your thinking, and allow silence in.

I always tell all my authors and writers to stop all the input into their busy brains. We are all so busy all the time, pushing data into our brains. We are making small talk, watching Netflix, listening to podcasts and radio shows. We are reading, studying and listening. Even when driving in the car – those blessed moments of potential silence – we are making calls, blasting music or engaging with talk radio or a podcast. We seldom allow silence and emptiness. And yet it is in the silence that truth and creativity lie. When you constantly fill your brain with other people's thoughts, you become an echo chamber of the mundane.

Turn off all the podcasts, stop the masterclasses and allow the deep well of silence to feed you.

My way of accessing silence is to walk in the mountains or run – with the silence as my only friend.

Gate 4: Practice deep listening

How shall there be redemption and resurrection unless there has been great sorrow? And isn't struggle and rising the real work of our lives?
— Mary Oliver, *Winter Hours*

There is a far greater intelligence than you in the quiet spaces.

This gate invites you to listen deeply to it. But it is only in these quiet spaces that we can sit still enough to hear. It was only when Inanna was hanging in the deep silence of the underworld that she could hear the message of what is eternal.

When you stop all other input, your own voice may become sharper and clearer. This was the deep quiet of the No Mind Meditation, that place where the mind is empty and open.

Follow the light and the signs.

Gate 5: Make new vows

He who learns must suffer. And even in our sleep pain, which cannot forget, falls drop by drop upon the heart, until in our own despair, against our will, comes wisdom through the awful graces of God.
– William Kent Krueger, *Ordinary Grace*

Make new promises. You can call these intentions or affirmations or simply dreams.

This gate asks you to find these powerful lights that pull you forward into a future and hold you to your deeper course.

I am going to suggest that these are bigger ones than before, wiser ones and richer ones.

The vows I made were simple ones.

I choose love over fear.

I stay open-hearted to life.

I say yes to life.

Speak them out loud, write them up. Prayer is so important. It matters not to whom or to what you pray, but what is important is to speak these higher desires and give them form and voice. It is seldom enough to think them, as thoughts are as transient as the wind. There is power in saying them, and writing them.

Open the seven gates

Gate 6: Cross the threshold in the new

It costs so much to be a full human being that there are few who have the enlightenment, or the courage to pay the price . . . One has to abandon altogether the search for security and reach out to the risk of living with both arms. – Morris L. West, *The Shoes of the Fisherman*

Start living into the future.

This gate invites you to take some very real actions that will move you into the future. This is really about doing the work in life. It goes beyond affirmations or intentions, and into taking deliberate and careful action to write a new story of your life.

Aside from the inner work, these are the things that pull you out of old patterns and behaviours, and into new choices.

Gate 7: Trust in grace

This is the world. Beautiful and terrible things will happen. Don't be afraid. – Frederick Buechner

This is perhaps the toughest gate to open. It is the gate of trust.

This gate asks you to know deeply that your life is guided and is unfolding in a divine way. Bad things will happen. Good things will happen. This is all part of the human condition. Centuries ago, the Sumerians knew this when the told the story of the great Queen of the Heavens who was stripped of all she held dear.

Just before I fell sick Llewelyn and I had sat late one night chatting. He had taken my hand then and looked me in the eyes. 'It's all going to go exactly according to plan,' he said. 'And we have no control whatsoever.'

Village of mystics and magic

It's 7 am on a Monday and the church bells are ringing. They count out the time in methodical chants. It is my wake-up call every single morning, except for Sundays, when they only start at eight. It's a small concession because then they chime like a non-stop drill call, rounding up the devout to church. That would not be me. I am the one burrowing deeper into my duvet and hoping someone brings me a coffee very soon.

But it's 7 am on a Monday and I know I must get up soon enough. The week must start. Very soon I will wake up my children and start the morning hustle. We will move from breakfast to brushing teeth to sending them on their way to the local Greek school for the day. It will not happen without a fight. It rarely happens without tears – either one of them or me. But now I have 30 minutes to just lie in the half-dream place. I have this time to slip between reality and unreality and between worlds.

This is the place I can find my love. My husband. He's been dead for a year now. But with my eyes closed and in the warm comfort below my sheets he is lying right behind me. His warm chest is against my back, and he is tucked in behind me holding me tight. His hand snakes down my side and settles on my butt. He gives it a squeeze. He loves my ass.

I can smell his heavy sleep against my neck and hear the gentle harrumph he makes in the pause between breaths. If I let him, I know his hand will move lower, and slip between my legs. I may just pretend to be asleep still, so he thinks it's a private caress.

I drink the moment in. This is where I want to be. Back with him.

Village of mystics and magic

This is the place I know best. This quiet feeling of completion with my husband behind me and our children still sleeping in their rooms. It all feels so right.

Except none of it is real.

He is gone. He is dead. 'Dead' is a hard word to say, so I use the word gone. It sounds as if he may just come back. But he won't.

Death is such an unexpected experience. I don't care how long you know someone is dying for; it is still a very physical shock when they are simply no longer there. Intellectually, I knew he was going to die. But I never thought he would simply not be there for a call, a cup of coffee, a chat or a giggle.

Death is just a word. The reality is harder. It took months for the physical loss of him to sink in.

He is gone forever. Gone because, despite all my attempts to find solace in the idea of a life after death, that is all I know right now.

He is just fucking gone.

No trace.

What am I actually doing here? What was I thinking? Why have I left behind everything that was safe and comfortable and soft and stifling and suffocating?

Why have I left everything I know and uprooted my children to follow my crazy adventure to an island that is so remote it's a speck on a speck on Google Earth?

And can I find home in a place like this? Am I totally crazy?

I am looking for something. Something I couldn't find in the comfort of the folks I knew. Something I found during my soul travels.

I have spent my life searching for meaning in all sorts of sacred places. So perhaps I do have a fighting chance finding it here.

So, I slip out of the comfort of my memories. They do not serve me right now. I put them away for another day.

'What on earth are you doing in Greece?' a friend asked me earlier in a short message. She had somehow missed my farewell and regular blog updates on my life on the island. 'Are your kids coping? I mean, why didn't you come to Sheffield? There are stacks of English schools? It would have been so much easier to live here.'

Yes. I could have made a more sensible choice. Most notably, a place where English was spoken.

It is hard on my kids. It is hard to try to start school. It is so hard on them that I am in danger of being taken away by child welfare and put on a poster for bad parenting decisions.

My friend Vicky gives me sage advice on a call. 'Steel is forged in fire,' she says. 'You are all going to be amazing people from everything you have been through.'

She is also the one who told me to reverse-perm my hair when we were sixteen so I have to take the good advice with the bad.

I solicit advice from all quarters. It's one of my weaknesses, and my strengths. I gather advice from friends, I hear what they think of what I have done, and what I am going to do. And then do my own thing regardless. It's not that I don't value advice. I absolutely do. I soak it up. Then I throw out the stuff that doesn't feel right to me, and stick with the stuff that lights up my centre.

I call Niall – the one I trust to deal me straight.

I am also fishing for some sympathy.

His voice crackles from a trip up to the Botswanan bush.

'This is too hard,' I tell him. 'I feel like I have had my adventure. I think I am ready to come home.'

'Forget it,' he tells me. 'You went to Greece to fulfil some deeper calling. You went to find something you were looking for. You are there, now you need to stick it out. Don't come home yet. You are not ready.'

He was right.

I came for a million good reasons

I came to get out of the rat race of a life I felt I was no longer a part of.

I came to break out of the system that starts a child at school at

Village of mystics and magic

age four and holds them there at a desk for six hours a day until they are eighteen.

I came because I felt like I wanted a different life.

I came because I nearly lost my life and somehow my old life didn't fit my skin any more.

I came because I lost my husband and that entire life was now over.

I wanted to mark that the one life I had lived had ended and that I was ready to live into the next one.

So, I came for a load of really rational and solid reasons. But I came for one simple, impossibly relentless call as well.

Have more fun.

Choose love and above.

The three words I took with me would not leave me. The ones whispered into my ear after an otherworldly kiss on my brow.

I did it because I wanted to honour that. I was searching how to live that, still.

I had found these things in the wild bush, in spirit worlds during my coma, and in deep silence of the meditations on the olive farm. I wanted to see where else I would find them. I knew it wasn't in the safe and ordinary life I had lived for the past 36 years. It simply wasn't there yet.

And so I came chasing it on a crazy path lit by ideas and courage.

'Remember your prayers,' Niall told me.

That morning I drive out into the empty farmlands alone. I find the right sticks and the right sand and gather them. I am going to make a new shrine. Out there in the fields between the goats I kneel down, and put my hiyas on.

I touch my forehead to the soil and I offer tobacco to the land.

Then I start to clap.

I sit there and I call on the ancestors in the ritual way. First, I call on my own family ancestors, grannies and grandpas who left long

LOVE AND ABOVE

ago. Then I call on the ancestors of the soil and the land. I call on the ancestors of the water and the sea. I call on the ancestors of the air.

I call on the elemental forces and the beings who watch over me.

I call on all of them as messengers to carry my prayers to God. I call on creation. I call on Llewelyn. I call them all to listen to my prayers and my blessings.

I know now that there is a greater power than me and I honour it in my way.

I notice as I speak out loud that a rhythm and a chant have risen in my pahla, and that I am clapping and weaving after every line. A heat is rising in me. I smile at this.

It is like a song and prayer and a blessing, all at once.

I take the sticks home and later make a small prayer shrine, just like the one at my home in Cape Town.

Cold winter for Shirley Valentine

I have an admirer in the village. Nikos the goat farmer.

He lives next door and drives a red truck.

The admiration started during a semi-naked tanning session in my courtyard. The winter sun peeked out and finally there was a bit of heat. It was too cold to pull on an actual bikini so I slipped off my leggings and lay in the sun in my knickers reading a book.

My rented house, and all village houses, has an enclosed courtyard. It is the only outdoor space, really, and the gate is for privacy, and also 'to keep the gypsies out', I was told.

I lay soaking up the first rays of sun and Vitamin D after a long winter and reading my Kindle when a cold shadow loomed over me and cut off my delicious sun.

'Scoot,' I told one of the kids.

Then I saw the dirty boots.

I flipped over fast and slipped my leggings back on over my skimpy thong.

Nikos was smiling widely. In his hands was a dead fish. Truthfully, it was neatly sliced and gutted and sitting on an oven tray amid potatoes, rosemary and onions. They were all raw.

He was talking fast and loudly in Greek, his hands gesticulating.

I was understanding none of it, and still wondering how much of my ass he had actually seen and just how long he had been there.

'Ela, ela etho.' He was pulling me now towards the gate.

'Ruby! Jude!' I yelled. 'Come here.'

Both the kids dropped their iPads and rushed out of the house as he started pulling me onto the road.

LOVE AND ABOVE

'Mom, I think he wants you to go into his kitchen.' Ruby's Greek was the best of all of ours. 'It's something about his oven.'

That made sense. He was holding an oven tray in his hands.

'Right! Both of you come with me, and bring my phone,' I demanded. 'This is a bit scary and I don't want to go into his house alone.'

So, the three of us followed him down the road. He opened his door and let us into his house. It was dark and empty and we inched behind him as he stalked through it. There was no furniture in the rooms and all the blinds were closed.

'Mom, this is creepy,' Ruby said.

'Nonsense,' I reassured her. 'It's a lovely space and I am sure he is a lovely man. Just lonely.'

We turned the corner and emerged into a huge kitchen. It was modern and shiny, totally inconsistent with the dark damp in the rest of the house.

Sitting in the middle was a brand new, state-of-the-art, never-been-used Smeg oven. He pulled me over to it and put the tray of fish into the oven, gesturing to the controls.

'I think he doesn't know how to work it,' I said to the kids. I knew a few things about ovens, most often that you need the timer to work to start the heat. It had an array of buttons and digital controls that flummoxed even me.

He had prepared a feast, and he had no idea how to cook it.

'Just Google it, Mom,' Jude said, 'and let's get out of here. It smells funny – like goats.'

I pulled out my phone and got online and pulled up the Smeg model and instructions. Five minutes later the oven was on, and the timer set for 45 minutes on rapid cook. We equally rapidly left the house and Nikos to his meal of fish.

'I think he wants us to stay and eat with him,' Ruby said. 'And I don't know if he can use that oven by himself. Mom. You may have to

Cold winter for Shirley Valentine

help him every time.'

It was the start of a long and unwelcome village courtship. Small gifts would be left on my steps at least once a week. Some cucumbers. A fish. Pastries. Then two metal containers of goat's milk. Unsure how to handle such a substance, I made hot chocolate with it that was promptly poured down the drain.

The next week I was having a coffee at the plateia when three of the women of the village came up and circled me.

'Ai, Sara. Be careful of that Nikos,' the one said. 'He's trellos,' she said, making the universal sign with her finger for crazy.

'Simple,' the other one whispered.

'He was married once. When she left him he tracked her down and one night he circled her house with cucumbers.'

'Malaka.'

I scribbled my new words down.

There are some phrases that are essential to learn when living on a Greek island.

Malaka is one of them.

But the three I needed to learn the most form the foundation of Greek culture:

σιγά-σιγά (sigá-sigá, pronounced 'cigar cigar'). This means 'slowly, slowly'.

isos αύριο (isos ávrio). This means 'maybe tomorrow'.

τι να κάνουμε (ti na kánoume). This means 'what to do . . .'.

The last one is the most frequently usedvc. It is not used as a question but as a statement. As in:

Sarah: Are you sure the post from my mother is not here? She sent it three weeks ago.

Postmaster: (Shrug) What to do. (Often followed by another shrug and 'isos ávrio'.)

The kids were leaps ahead of me in learning Greek and Ruby was picking it up fast at the Greek school in the village.

It's hard to be a hippy with kids

Greece was not what they expected. When we first arrived and Jude saw all the old stone buildings, he burst into tears.

'Where are the white buildings? Where are the *Mamma Mia!* singers?'

'Oh Jude,' Ruby told him. 'We will find all the singers in the morning. It's too late now for anyone to be out.' She reached out and hugged him.

'We are going to have such fun, my boy, don't you worry,' she said. I watched her brave little face. Just ten years old and she knew what to say and do. She glanced at me, and we made a silent pact to hold it together.

Now we are settled into village life.

Last week Ruby came to me to have A Very Serious Talk. She had tears in her eyes. She explained that Greek kids do not take packed lunches to school and that it's frankly embarrassing to pull out a lunchbox with fruit and 'homemade sandwiches'. They all buy their school lunches from the bakery on the way to school and she doesn't fit in with this Woolies lunchbox.

She is at school, Jude stays at home, close to me, all day. If I even walk to the shops he will come with and cannot let me out of his sight.

I have to be wary of the sources of information. The old man down the road has a shop. It is sort of a clothing/haberdashery/sewing shop under his house. Everything is an inch deep in dust, but it is the only place I can find stuff that doesn't come from China. Shopping there takes time as things are in big piles. I love that kind of shop.

The kids refuse to go in because they think it's creepy.

It's hard to be a hippy with kids

He taught me that 'son' is 'illios'. The lesson involved pointing to Jude, as well as gestures of the sun shining, suntan oil, heat and pointing to the many religious symbols on the wall.

I have been using that word for Jude ever since. Yesterday one of the parents politely told me that 'illios' actually means 'Son of God'.

A village means you mix with people from every sphere of life.

In the small village of Eresos, 1 000 are elderly – that leaves a remainder of 500 between the ages of 18 and 40. The number who speak English is possibly 30, so your actual choice for friends is very thin.

Some of the kids at the school come from gypsy families, remote farms, absolute poverty, or have no parents.

I was driving Ruby and a friend to the beach, and I asked the girl who the man was on the motorbike.

'He seems so friendly,' I said. 'He is always smiling and winking at me.'

'Oh yeah, he's the drug dealer,' said the then-ten-year-old Ismini. 'He's just back after being in prison on Chios. The winking is his code if you want to buy gear.'

Right, then.

One of the friends had a very glamorous mother. She walked up and down the main road and side roads all day pushing a bike. Most often her skin had a sheen of oil. She was very sexy and wore skin-tight white leggings that were ever so slightly transparent in the sun as she bent over her bike.

'Who's that?' I asked a friend the one morning. 'She's so pretty.'

'Oh, she's the village whore,' said Saloni.

'Mom, those pants are tight, eh? She's got a camel toe,' said Jude. 'What's a whore?'

Ah, we sigh. Village life!

That's the catchphrase we use to explain the strange world of a tiny Greek village.

LOVE AND ABOVE

No water? Village life!

Being chased by a ram? Village life!

Chatting to the drug dealer as you both wait for your kids to finish football? Village life!

Today the priest from the small church down the road walked past in his long black gown. There are three churches in the village, and you can choose allegiance.

'Kalimera padre.'

Worried that was actually Latin, I switched back to English, corrected myself and said 'brother'.

'No, Mom. Isn't that for a monk?' Ruby hissed. So, I corrected again and just said 'hi'.

Kalimera. Good morning.

That is a hold-all and another essential word to know and use.

He was having a chuckle. 'Ja-sou Zara, are you coming to church mass? For Easter?'

I nodded. 'Sigora.' Definitely.

The good news is that church is literally the only place in Greece you cannot smoke.

We survived our first Greek Easter. Not with a sugar hangover like you would expect, but some sort of 48-hour post-celebratory spiritual slump. It was a push to the finish, but worth it in terms of general spiritual fitness and village joie de vivre. It started at 2 pm on Good Friday, with the church bells chiming for a full hour with varying levels of speed and tone.

Then the music started coming over the village on a loudspeaker. The fireworks started as it got dark.

'This is so fun!' Jude screeched as another huge explosion went off just outside out gate. It was a group of snickering boys. The next one was an apple stuffed with some explosive device they lobbed into our yard, giggling.

'Mom, can I go with the boys?' Jude asked. 'Please?'

It's hard to be a hippy with kids

He had barely left my side in months, and this was an opportunity I could not resist, despite it being a dangerous one.

Minutes later he was back.

'I need ten euro to buy some poppers.'

I raised my eyes as I fished in my wallet.

'You sure that was the name?'

In my day, poppers were a different kind of bang.

He shrugged.

'Be careful,' I started to call, but I corrected myself fast.

'Have fun!' I called instead.

'Have a blast!' Ruby called, and we both chuckled.

Summer life's a beach

Greek islands during summer are like a cabaret that has just had the stage lights turned on.

Summer is Showtime. Ta daaaaa!

All the drab clothes come off and the glitter and sequins are put on. The tiny beach towns come alive, shimmering with anticipation. Every bar and restaurant owner spends the weeks after 1 May, Spring Day, getting ready to open in June. The long wooden planks are dusted off and laid out as the beach decks start taking form.

As the tiny tendrils of summer started growing, the Osho Centre started to clean and get ready to open. It was the first stirring that things were starting to change. I got a text from my friends: *Come beloved. Please join us. Spring is here and we are celebrating on May 1. We have some fresh strawberries and we will make flower garlands and celebrate.*

Suddenly everyone was busy and the lethargy of winter was gone.

The village shops start moving their stock from the upper (winter) village down to the summer one. Shelf by shelf, the supermarkets and pharmacies move down. Slowly, small traders come from Athens, Thessaloniki and mainland Greece. Beautiful shops open their windows, packed with Turkish fabrics and jewellery.

Restaurants fill their planters with flowers. Lights are hung off every roof and shutters are painted a fresh coat of Aegean blue. Empty shops are stocked and opened. The leaves, creepers and weeds filling the streets are cleared. Streetlights are turned on. It's tourist season and the islands have about three months to make their income for the entire year.

Our lease had ended at the first house, so we found one near the

Summer life's a beach

beach.

We had a string of visitors all summer. Harry joined us from the small English seaside town of Felixstowe as our au pair.

Liz and her new boyfriend Mendez were there for a few months, so we had family around. Then the girls arrived, and the Triumvirate was reunited; we spent late nights laughing in the beachfront bars.

Most nights we would eat souvlaki and sit on the street or down by the beach until late. We only seemed to get to bed around midnight most nights, and the kids were getting used to the late summer nights.

We'd come a long, long way since those early days in the dark of winter. The kids are relaxed and they roam free most of the day. They do check in with me every few hours, but the kids here play on the beach until late at night. I had to let the kids run wild a lot because I had a lot of work to do, running a magazine online and editing books.

I decided in the late summer to invite some writers to join me and write their books.

I found a venue that seemed so right: a run-down but bohemian hotel just on the edge of the Kampos. That is the space where the beach villas end, and the real farmlands begin. It felt like the perfect place to bring writers from all over the world.

'Don't expect fancy,' I told them in the first welcome email when they enquired about the retreat. 'This is not the village for that! It is the place for crystal-clear seas, naked beaches and lesbians.'

I am not sure my marketing efforts were that successful as only four writers finally turned up. One, it seemed, had been more enticed by the naked beaches and lesbians than the writing.

During the day the writing group gathered, and we sat, wrote and shared our writing and our memories. Others joined the group. A stray cat climbed onto someone's lap. A glass of wine slipped into another's hand. Time stretched and bent as we sat and wrote and wrote.

The lesbian festival organiser

Imagine about eight hundred lesbians from all over Europe coming for fourteen days of parties.

During the last months of the summer, I put my journalistic and marketing skills to work and worked on the International Women's Festival, an annual event and lesbian festival that runs for two weeks every September.

I joined the month before to help, and worked on the logistics and then the actual event. The packed festival office was filled with straight and trans people, queens and drama queens, big fights, screaming Italians, screaming Greeks, lots of laughter, make-up and the occasional hairdresser with a teasing comb.

The kids were still on their endless three-month summer holiday, so most often they were in the office too. Nobody can claim these two were not getting a very broad education.

'That's my mom. She not actually a lesbian,' I heard Ruby telling one visitor as she clamped on her festival wristband.

Ruby helped with the ticket sales and general information. Jude was the errand boy, racing around dropping off posters, cables and freddo cappuccinos on his bike all day.

'Mom, it's not exactly the same as *Mamma Mia!*,' Jude said late one night as we sat singing on the beach around a fire. 'But it's not as bad as I first thought.'

We had been swimming all day and jumping off rocks into the sea. Our hair was bleached white by the salty sea and even his eyebrows were a white slash against his golden skin.

He was lying against me, and we were watching the fire and the

The lesbian festival organiser

musicians. The sound of music from the beach bars floated towards us and mixed with the gentle lap of waves.

I leaned against him and watched the sky.

Was it almost a year ago I had pulled that small and broken boy out of school? That boy stricken with panic attacks, who could not be away from me for a second?

Was it just a year before that I had been dancing up at the olive groves of Afroz, with a broken rib?

That day, he had been racing on the beach with friends. I noticed how he would still check on me all day, but slowly, slowly, he could make up more distance from me.

Was it a year before that, that I was fighting for my life?

In July, Ruby turned eleven. I was preparing a slide show, cards, songs and a big party. I opened my photos and took a look at what was.

Sometimes this thing called grief just hits so hard and fast, and you can't control it. Lots of the time I can stop it. And sometimes I don't want to stop it. I just want to feel it again so I can reconnect and remind myself that it is still a part of me. And also that the love is still there.

In a heartbeat, the two years of survival were wiped out and I was back . . . right back in the death. I always got stuck there. In the last month of his life. I couldn't get beyond that, back further.

I couldn't get back to the good times we had. All that played, over and over and over again, was me leaving him, the struggle in the last months as he lost control of his body, and the awful last few days.

Death can be like that. We get caught in the trauma moment.

Minutes turned into hours as I got lost in the past.

I wanted to go home now. I was ready. Done.

My older and wise sister Trish was visiting, and we sat in the plateia over a dinner of grilled lamb chops, tzatziki, steamed horta, thick-cut potato chips and salad.

'We miss you all,' I said. 'I have learnt a lot of things over the past

LOVE AND ABOVE

few months of living alone, just us in a tiny house on a tiny island. One of these things is that you can't always go with a feeling. The feeling passes. And then the sun comes out and it all feels a bit better.'

'We miss you all too, but this is a good thing you are doing here,' Trish said. 'It is small and safe and I can see the kids are starting to gain confidence again.'

I nodded. 'I came here for a reason and I mustn't lose sight of that. We came here to heal together, and to find a new story for our lives without Llew. We couldn't do that trapped in the old story of our lives.'

I knew I was also looking for something I couldn't find for myself, or my family, back in the ordinary. I was living out the promise. I was searching for a quality I had long since lost. Joy.

'I am having ups and downs, but in between it all I am stripping away my old identity and creating a new one.'

Walking home along the cobbled streets, we stopped and looked up at the stars.

The Greek musician

It was almost time to go home. Our year was almost up, and our tickets booked.
The Lesbian Festival was in full swing and we decided to have a party at the hotel where I had run the writing retreat.

'Come and jam with us tonight,' a Dutch author and friend, Karin Giphart, asked. She was part of a couple and a duet with singer Michelle Courtens.

'We want Ruby to sing. We will have wine and all sing and celebrate.'

Ruby was born with a voice from the angels, pitch perfect, rich and deep – it was something spectacular.

It was dreamy and hot as we wound up the paved streets and past the small chapel, where we stopped to light a candle and send a blessing. The music had already started, and a group of friends and musicians sat in the rooftop gardens as the bar opened and wine was uncorked. My sister Trish was there, and my niece Kate joined.

Michelle's voice soared out over the village as we joined in, drumming or listening to the magic of her voice. Ruby's clear, beautiful voice joined in.

'We invited our sound engineer, Mike,' Michelle said. 'He's an amazing guitarist and singer. You must know him? He lives in the village.'

I frowned. 'Not sure. I may.'

'Ah, Mike,' she said, and jumped up to hug someone as he walked through the door.

The low-lit courtyard was twinkling with fairy lights and the candles that were dotted around.

He walked through the door and into the light.

Ah heavens.

As I saw him my heart near skipped a beat.

Dark skin, darker hair and a wide, white smile that slashed his face with joy.

Dimples.

He was not tall, but solid and real, as if he had been moulded from the Greek sun.

He moved through the room and greeted everyone, a warm and easy smile lighting his brown eyes.

I knew him. My being knew him, and a smile spread across my face. I could not hold it in. Sheer and utter joy.

Here you are.

The one I have been waiting for all this time.

In the two years since Llew had died I had not loved anyone. In the year since I had moved to Greece I hadn't touched anyone, despite all the magic and dance at the Osho Centre.

I was there to heal and be whole, and romance wasn't part of that. My soul simply was not ready, and I hadn't wanted to equate love with a man.

The love and joy I was chasing was bigger, broader and more vast than a person. But now, just as I was about to leave, this walked through the door and up to me.

'I have seen you and the kids around,' he smiled.

'You have?' I could hardly keep the shine from my eyes.

'For sure. This is a small village and I see you around. I have even chatted to you all a few times up at Caféne.'

'Okay, sorry, I don't know if I remember.'

He smiled a lazy, sexy, wicked grin and nodded. 'That's okay, we Greeks all look the same!'

We laughed.

The Greek musician

If you believe in past lives, this was a past life talking to me.

You, it said. *After all this time, I see you again.*

I pushed it aside, and put it down to hormones. Hot and raging ones. So, I shook off my scarf and let my skin feel the air.

Then he took out his guitar and sat down and started to play. He sang Greek songs and rock songs. Ruby sang with him, and I watched his patient strumming, letting her keep the beat.

More and more people joined our party as we sang. A joint was passed around. The kids decided to walk home and go play on the beach as it was late.

Finally, the cooler sea breeze moved across the fields. I moved away from the singing, to the cooler side, where the wind was catching the reeds over the bar. He came and stood next to me, leaning on the bar counter as he took out his tobacco and rolled a cigarette.

'Alpha beer,' he told Vaso behind the bar, then took out his wallet to pay.

I put my hand on his. It was hard with callouses on the palm.

'Put that away, I am buying you this one. Thank you for the music. It has been the most magical evening.'

Oh but the smell of him. I wanted to drink it in, dive into his neck and breathe so deeply. It was as if his skin simply smelled of the sea and the sun.

Kate walked up to me later, my eyes dreamy as I watched him play.

'He's hot,' she said.

'So hot.'

'I saw him looking at you.'

I grinned.

'Oh yes,' she laughed. 'I think it's a yes.'

Kate turned to me. 'Sarah! Go with him.'

I laughed. 'Not tonight. I will. But not tonight.'

'What makes you think you will see him again?'

LOVE AND ABOVE

'Oh, I have a feeling . . . I also know he is playing with the band on Thursday night,' I grinned. 'At Flamingo.'

'Oh Sar, you need to kiss him before you leave. This is the island of love.'

We giggled.

'I think I just will,' I said.

The next day I took them to the airport and turned back on the long drive to the village. I knew he was waiting. I wasn't sure what he was waiting for, but I knew it was something.

Two days later, on Thursday, I walked to the Flamingo Bar just as the band was starting. I joined a table of friends and sat back. He was there, standing behind the desk, mixing the sounds.

When the last song ended, he came and joined our table and we all sat having a beer and laughing.

He turned to me, taking my hand and mixing his fingers with mine. The delicious heat spread through them.

'So, do you want to do something?'

I nodded. 'Yeah. Definitely.'

'Well, we can go for a cocktail, or we can go out to sea on my boat.'

I couldn't stop the smile. The joy. The delight. The adventure.

'Let's go out to sea on your boat,' I said.

We left the small harbour and raced out into the Aegean Sea. The salt stung my cheeks and I dipped my hand into the warm water.

We picked up speed and a laugh of joy ripped out me. I felt him smile next to me and laugh. The wind was pulling my hair and chasing the breath from my mouth. I wanted to kiss him, and now. We were going so fast we could not speak, just catch the wind, and the swell, and laugh.

A bit later – or was it hours? – we dropped anchor and the boat settled into a steady rise and fall. We didn't speak and just sat for a while, feeling the sea beneath us. We were far away from the village now

The Greek musician

and even the twinkling lights had faded.

Then we pulled off our clothes and dove into the clear sea. It was warm and I closed my eyes and swam deeper and deeper.

We both laughed from the carefree joy of that.

I lay on my back and looked up at the stars. A blanket of twinkling lights lay above us and I knew, as I lay there in the cool ocean, that he was smiling down at me.

I had his blessing for this moment. This love. This moment in time. This was what being alive was.

Finally, salty and naked, we climbed back onto the boat.

He kissed me then, his hot mouth devouring me as our salty tongues met. I felt alive, my body singing with the sting of the salt and the delicious smell enveloping me as his hot skin pressed again mine.

We just tasted and touched each other. Fast the first time. Then slower.

We pulled jackets on and sat and rolled a cigarette. I didn't smoke, but it felt like the right thing to do.

It may have been two in the morning when we pulled back into the tiny harbour and he dropped me at home. I skipped to the door, my hair stiff with salt, my lips bruised from his and my heart so full of delight and the delicious connection.

'Where the hell have you been?'

The porch light went on and Ruby stood glaring at me.

I choked back a laugh, realising I was a bit unsteady on my feet from the rocking of the boat as I walked towards her.

'Just out on a boat with a friend,' I said, and kissed her on the top of her head.

At all of eleven, she turned and went straight back to sleep.

I sat on the porch with a cup of tea to watch the sun rise a few hours later. I remembered sitting on another porch, watching the sun rise. It seemed like a lifetime ago that I had walked out after the headache had first struck.

LOVE AND ABOVE

I was a very long way away from that person. At the time, I thought I knew how life worked. I was caught in one myth.

I believed that marriage and children were my path. That we would grow old together and have grandchildren. We were making and earning and being fabulous.

I didn't yet know that we have many lives in one lifetime. That was just one of mine. I was creating a new one, and there may be more to come.

Back then, on that other porch, I didn't know there were sacred waterfalls and magical places.

I didn't know that I could soar through the universe.

I didn't know that life and death were so close

I didn't know that I could dance in the wilderness and feel my heart expand.

I didn't know that joy was so close and so easy.

I thought we were young and invincible and that the future was certain.

Two nights later, I went out with Mike again. Even though we were headed home to Cape Town, I called an estate agent the next day and found a house in the winter village and signed a year's rental.

In my heart, I knew that this story wasn't ready to be over yet. I knew we had a few more summers in Greece and more adventures to go on.

The path of love

For so many years I have been searching. For what? you may ask. This is something I ask myself so many times in so many ways.

I searched in sweat lodges and wild expanses, and on dance floors. I searched at the bottom of wine bottles. I searched in yoga, in therapy, in trance tents, in breathwork, tantra and in Zen Buddhism.

You see, that's the hard thing. It is easier, perhaps, to look when you know what you are looking for. But I have always had this feeling. This longing for . . .

Something bigger. A reconnection.

In all these years of gurus and sangoma trips and breakdowns and breakups and chanting and Osho and God knows what other batshit wonderful and crazy stuff I have done.

I touched it. Joy. Peace. Love

Something quietly, deeply and slowly happened.

It's probably just called getting older, but it feels much easier to find now. I just have to remember it.

Maybe it's some reward for just staying here and playing in this crazy thing called life.

So often people say to me, Sarah, what a time you have had. You are so brave. Or they talk about how traumatised I must be. How dreadful. How lonely. But most of me doesn't really understand what on earth they are talking about.

It has allowed me to work in the field I do, working with authors and helping them tell their own stories. It has allowed me to study mythology and start to see the myths we live out. Because when life happens, it just happens, and are you in it. This *is* life, I want to shout.

LOVE AND ABOVE

This.

This is what post-traumatic bliss is. It is wild and expansive and full. It is terrible and beautiful.

I spent a huge part of the past decade having regrets and wishing I had been a different person, done things differently, been kinder, nicer, wiser, bigger. I have replayed moments in my mind and things I have said – and I would have done anything, once, to change some of these.

But now I look at my life and no longer feel that way. It was all meant to be. It was all part of the game and part of the gift.

I know we have many lives to live, and that we sometimes hold on too tight to one that no longer fits us.

I absolutely know that life is guided. Mine is. Yours is.

The Resurrection Plant

Niall and I are walking on the hill that leans over the river in Botswana. We stop at the evergreen olive tree and scramble up above the rocks. This is the place where the Naked Man was hiding and where Llewelyn found it one night after a dream.

We scattered his ashes there a year after he died and now we are back, close to a decade later.

The tree the green plant was nestled in has died. Still, at the base of the dead tree a very small part of the plant remains, clinging on to life.

I bend down and touch it, running my fingers down the spongy exterior.

This is the place where his ashes lie, just above the river that flows in summer. As I sift through the baked sand I see some of his bones still there. Just small shards and fragments lying in the ground where we scattered them so long ago. I pick one up – the size of a pip – and hold it tight.

We sit down for a while. We place snuff on the ground and we pahla and talk to him. We tell him about our lives, and I tell him that the kids are well, and what they are up to. I tell him that they are older now, almost adults. They are strong and special and full of inquiry.

I tell him that Ruby has his legs and his confidence, and that Jude has his love of photography and noir films. I tell him that I am good, that I have made it.

We sit for a long while and listen to the wind in the dry grass and the thorns.

I place the bone shard back down on the ground.

LOVE AND ABOVE

'Bye, my prince,' I say.

A bit later we wander back down the hill and through the dry riverbed as the sun rises higher. Soon it will be too hot to be out in the bush and my fair skin is already flushed and pricking in the heat.

'This summer the rain will come, and this will all be full and flowing again,' Niall tells me as we stop in the riverbed. He is gathering herbs and plants for medicines, and he has a bag that is slowly filling. We amble along, slow and steady. No hurry.

As we walk along the path and through the scratchy thorns and grass, something catches my eye, waving at me from just a few metres back in the grasses.

I walk over and lean down next to a dried-out and black bush. It looks like it has been burned by fire.

'What's this plant?' I ask.

He nods and smiles at me.

'We call it Vuka. The Resurrection Plant. "Vukabafile" in Tswana means "awaken the dead".'

He hands me the knife.

'Cut some.'

I cut off a large branch of it and look at it closely.

'I think this is your plant,' he says.

The Resurrection Plant.

AFTERWORD - A NEW CANCER JOURNEY

This book covers about four years of my life, from age 32 to 38, and the events that happened in that time. Ruby has now left school and Jude will soon. They are grown and powerful and real young adults, ready to change the world,

Back then, after we left that summer, we went back to Greece and lived there for another three years.

We walked in the mountains, gathered rosemary and herbs and dried them. We went for long bike rides. I bought an old car, and we took the occasional drive around the island, visited the hot springs or went for a lunch at a taverna a few hours away.

I homeschooled the kids (very badly), making sure they wrote their exams every year. At the same time, they attended the local village school where only Greek was spoken. They took their South African textbooks and did their own work during the day. I looked at their friends in South Africa and saw them doing six hours of school a day and then homework. We did a maximum of about five hours work a week, most often in a coffee shop or at the beach. We would whip through the concepts in the textbooks – solar system, Bartolomeu Diaz, solutions and solids, mixed algebra – now, time for a swim!

I edited a magazine, and more and more writers started to come to do writing retreats with me on the island.

Every day we woke at 7 am to the wild ringing of church bells. I settled down to work by 9 am after cleaning the house, and tried to finish by lunch when I grabbed a shopping basket and walked the two minutes to the school to collect the kids.

Between 2 pm and 5 pm a Greek village shuts down. My landlord explained that you *never* call a Greek person in this time (after my daily afternoon phone calls about heating, electricity or showers breaking).

LOVE AND ABOVE

At that time, he told me, 'Every Greek man is either sleeping or having sex.'

We spent a lot of time fishing. I had been dating Mike the Gorgeous Greek Musician for a while and he fished a lot. So, we would go out on many mornings really early, and he taught the kids to catch squid and then to bait larger fish. Sometimes we took the fish to a small taverna and sat by the sea and they cooked them for us and we ate them with a fresh salad and lots of ouzo.

Then everything changed again.

It was the lazy height of summer, and the air was buzzing with possibilities. Everything was good and we were packing to return home. Ruby needed to go to high school, and I could no longer homeschool her. We were all finally ready to let go of the island life and join the 'real world'.

My mother and Liz had just been to visit. I had just had another large group of writers come from all over the world to do a retreat with me, and they were leaving the next day. Our village house was packed and ready, and all that was left was a few days for cocktails, long walks and goodbyes.

I had packed up my shrine and returned the elements to the land.

I was living a new story. Far away was the sick and frail widow. Long gone was the powerful publisher. They were still a part of me, but in the past.

I was standing naked in my room after a cold shower, letting the hot breeze dry the water and bring down the summer heat. I started to feel my breasts. Standing in front of the mirror, I palmed them, felt their weight in my hands, and then let my fingers feel more closely. No real reason, just a sudden hunch.

My fingers went straight to a lump on the left one. The lump was hiding, just there, and it felt soft, but solid. My heart started thumping.

Cancer.

The word raced through my blood. I dropped my hand, terrified

Afterword - A new cancer journey

to even touch that small soft thing.

My rational mind told me to calm down. It is probably nothing, I told myself.

I felt the other one. No lump. Could I have imagined it?

No, it was there.

One thought. Cancer.

The day before I left the small village, I walked down the hot summer streets and through the winding alleyways and this incredible feeling of knowing came over me. I knew this lump was cancer. I knew the one thing I was most afraid of was actually happening to me.

And I knew I would be okay.

I remember the very moment the feeling descended on me. It flushed me from above like a gift from the heavens. It came as a voice as clear and loud as if someone had shouted it in my ear.

You will survive this, it said.

I closed my eyes in the heat and I was back there. Back there with the tribe of black women, singing to me and standing behind me.

My small family of three landed in Cape Town. I made small talk and smiled but inside I was twisted into knots of worry.

Mammogram

Ultrasound.

Cancer.

It had been a week since that deliciously warm summer's afternoon in Greece.

Cancer was the word I had avoided for four years.

I almost couldn't bear to hear it spoken. I ran from it. I wanted to keep it very far away from me. And now here it was, right on my own doorstep.

I told the kids what was going on and what I knew. Ruby was just thirteen and about to start high school. Jude was eleven. It just wasn't fair.

And the fear came rushing back. Waiting for results and doctors was filled with fear and anxiety. Waiting for the appointment, waiting for the test, waiting for the result. I was terrified. All the work, all the joy and all the struggle had been wiped out in one second – with one word.

But I wasn't the same person any more.

I understood, in that moment, that I could not live in the energy of fear. The only way to heal or get through this was to change again. I needed to raise my own vibration and my energy field again.

Every morning I moved my prayer in that way. I sat before my shrine or walked out onto the mountain and raised my vibrations with breath and meditation and chants.

I went back to an old favourite in Brandon Bays and The Journey work. I started to drop through these feelings. From fear into lower ones. Deeper ones. Lighter ones. This process works by dropping down into feelings until you reach bliss, joy and love – or Source. My visualisation was rising up into them.

Same thing, different words.

I had to work to crowd out those feelings. I worked at it every day, filling my body with the feeling of joy. I was finding it now – not just in wild space and in moments, but I was able to shift and create it in a meditation and in a moment.

I just had to remember it.

I tattooed the word 'joy' on my arm in Greek. Xara.

In the next few months of chemo, it was not always easy to feel the joy. Many times I fell back into fear or anxiety, loathing or despair. I felt disgusting, sick and shut down. I felt very sorry for myself. I felt so sorry for my family to have to go through this with me. I felt so scared that I might not survive, might leave my kids without any parents at all. I felt deeply the unfairness of it all. These were all easy to feel.

Mike the Gorgeous Greek came to support me, but our relationship couldn't last the cancer and he drifted away. And I let him go.

I was very, very sad. Sad for everything that had happened. Sad

Afterword - A new cancer journey

for myself. Sad for my children.

Sometimes I let myself feel the fear. I let it course through my body, I felt my pulse skitter and my heart pound. I let it run like wildfire. I made it deeper and richer and bigger. Like the gibberish or many of the other meditations I had done over the years at the Osho Centre. I welcomed it and felt it.

Then I let it go.

I picture a scene sometime in the future, in summer, with my love and the kids. We're all in the sun by the pool with a big roast planned for lunch. The kids are laughing, music is floating across the air and life is good. The feeling infuses my body. It lifts my soul and I start laughing. Just like that. Joy races through me. Love, fun and silliness. There is no place for anxiety. And the hours of MRIs or chemo just fly by.

Fear is not there for me any more. Sure, there are times when it comes rushing in, and these thoughts crowd my head and drag me down. But putting these thoughts aside is a choice I make again and again.

Every year I go to Greece for the summer, and take a group of authors and writers with me. I sign up for any adventure that takes me into a deeper and more real connection with life and joy.

I seek it out and I make it happen.

I choose love and above.

ACKNOWLEDGEMENTS

To my sisters Elizabeth (Lizzy), Jayne and Trish – for walking with me through this journey of life.

Mom, who has stood by my side holding my hand for my entire life, not just for those four weeks.

Ruby Roderick for your shining light.

Jude Roderick for your kind heart.

Ingrid and John Roderick, whose generosity of spirit have carried the torch. You have been there always and helped me raise these two beautiful children in the most magnificent way.

Kath Roderick for being the most loving sister to Llew and for becoming my sister and most special auntie.

Dad and Kath, my sister – both in heaven.

The band of brothers – Richard Kilpert, Daniel Isherwood and Ronald Wertlen.

The Triumvirate. My soul sisters Lulu Leach and Georgia Black, who are most desperately loved.

Niall Campbell for being a unique human, guide, keeper of the old ways and protector of tradition. But most of all, the best friend I could chose to hang with.

Dr Murray Rushmere – and the entire extended Rushmere clan of Grant, Tracy and Sarah, who were there all the way.

Laurika Rauch, Llew's open-hearted aunt, fellow artist and supporter.

Claudia Rauber and her incredible vision and life at Phakalane.

Colin Campbell, who teaches so deeply and richly.

Janine Ashworth, Joshua Hapgood and Enah, Boudewyn and Eleane Eras – for being the rock and support for our Jude (and me), and being part of our bigger extended family.

Acknowledgements

Kate Emmerson, my vision holder, business partner and wifey. Life is so much richer and deeper with you in it. And we laugh a lot too.

The Foot Club ladies, who listened to me and held and cried with me over all the years – Paola Wulfsohn, Helen Searra, Natalie Uren, Heather Creswell, Savannah Erasmus, Michelle Greenwood, Santa Gomez, Wendy Daffarn.

Victoria Asmussen Dekker, for being there first, last and always.

Llew's Crew, who formed such a tight circle around him from the start, at various points in life and all the way to the end – Marietjie and Roelof Oelofsen, PC and Mieke Janse van Rensburg, Erica and Manfred Klocke, Mathys Mocke, Daron and Laura Chatz, Sam Kelly, Simon Anderson, Karen Slater, Savannah Sefor, Mark Erasmus, David Shapshak, Wendy and Buster Sefor, Leah, Tamsen de Beer, the Wulfsohns, Natalie and Vincent Uren.

To all the doctors, healers and guides who played a role along the way.

The Camps Bay schools, and in particular Stuart Collier, Nancy Roussopoulos and Mr Von Ess.

The Osho Afroz Meditation Centre, and the small and magic community of sannyasins.

The village of Eressos. Most of all, the wonderful Joanna Savva and Wendy Jansen at Sappho Travel.

The International Eressos Women's Festival and all the singing friends I made along the way – Karin Giphart, Michelle Courtens, Lara A King and Nicky Mitchell.

Mike Glambedakis – for loving me and the kids through the summer, and the winter.

All my writers, who have inspired me over the years to be more open and vulnerable, and to share my own story.

Harry Lynch for your adventurer's heart.

Stephen Symons for his poetry and his Julie Etellin for always being there on the side and for sharing our boys.

LOVE AND ABOVE

Katherine-Mary Pichulik, for being a fellow soul traveller.

Gill Moodie, publisher extraordinaire and truth seeker – for believing in this story. And for all the laughs and shared cups of coffee in the canteens as journalists at *Mail & Guardian* then *Business Day*.

ABOUT THE AUTHOR

Sarah Bullen is an author, storyteller and much-loved international writing mentor with a unique brand of humour and heart. She runs writing mentorships, mystical storytelling retreats and women's rites of passages around the world. Her books include *Hey Baby! The Hip New Mom's Guide That's All About You* and *Write your Book in 100 Days! Stop Mucking About & Just Write Your Book*. She is a former journalist and magazine editor.

Find her at www.sarahbullen.com.

Printed by Amazon Italia Logistica S.r.l.
Torrazza Piemonte (TO), Italy